SRI RAMAKRISHNA

HIS LIFE AND SAYINGS

FRIEDRICH MAX MÜLLER

PEACOCK BOOKS

Published by
PEACOCK BOOKS
7/22, Ansari Road, Darya Ganj, New Delhi-110002
Tel.: +91-11-40775252, 40775214, 23273880, 23275880
Web: www.peacockbooks.com
E-mail: orders@atlanticbooks.com

Peacock Books is an imprint of
Atlantic Publishers and Distributors (P) Ltd.
Web: www.atlanticbooks.com

First Published 1898

Printed & bound in India by Atlantic Print Services

Friedrich Max Müller (1823–1900) was a renowned German philosopher and scholar of linguistics and oriental studies. Educated at the University of Leipzig and Oxford, he is best known for his pioneering work in the field of Indology and for translating and interpreting ancient texts from Sanskrit and other Indian languages. Müller played a significant role in bringing Hindu philosophy and spiritual teachings to the Western world, primarily through his work on the *Rigveda* and other key texts of Indian religion. His intellectual curiosity and scholarly depth led to his involvement in the translation of significant works such as *The Upanishads* and *The Bhagavad Gita*. A prominent advocate for the study of comparative religion, Müller contributed significantly to the understanding of Eastern spirituality and its teachings.

Noteworthy works by Max Müller:

- *The Upanishads* (1851)
- *History of Ancient Sanskrit Literature* (1859)
- *India, What Can It Teach Us?* (1867)
- *The Dhammapada* (1881)

Contents

Preface

The name of *Rāmakṛishna* has lately been so often mentioned in Indian, American, and English newspapers that a fuller account of his life and doctrine seemed to me likely to be welcome, not only to the many who take an interest in the intellectual and moral state of India, but to the few also to whom the growth of philosophy and religion, whether at home or abroad, can never be a matter of indifference. I have therefore tried to collect as much information as I could about this lately-deceased Indian Saint (died in 1886), partly from his own devoted disciples, partly from Indian newspapers, journals, and books in which the principal events of his life were chronicled, and his moral and religious teaching described and discussed, whether in a friendly or unfriendly spirit.

Whatever may be said about the aberrations of the Indian ascetics to whom *Rāmakṛishna* belonged, there are certainly some of them who deserve our interest, nay even our warmest sympathy. The tortures which some of them, who hardly deserve to be called *Saṃnyāsins*, for they are not much better than jugglers or *Hathayogins*, inflict on themselves, the ascetic methods by which they try to subdue and annihilate their passions, and bring themselves to a state of extreme nervous exaltation accompanied by trances or fainting fits of long duration, are well known to all who have lived in India and have become acquainted there not only with Rajahs and Maharajahs, but with all the various elements that constitute the complicated system of Indian society. Though some of the stories told of these martyrs of the flesh and of the spirit may be exaggerated, enough remains of real facts to rouse at all events our curiosity. When some of the true *Saṃnyāsins*, however, devote their thoughts and meditations to philosophical and religious problems, their utterances, which sway large multitudes that gather round them in their own country, cannot fail to engage our attention and sympathy, particularly if, as in the case of *Rāmakṛishna*, their doctrines are being spread by zealous advocates not only in India, but in America also, nay even in England.

We need not fear that the *Saṃnyāsins* of India will ever find followers or imitators in Europe, nor would it be at all desirable that they should, not even for the sake of Psychic Research, or for experiments in Physico-psychological Laboratories. But apart from that, a better knowledge of the teachings of one of them seems certainly desirable, whether for the statesmen who have to deal with the various classes of Indian society, or for the missionaries who are anxious to understand and to influence the inhabitants of that country, or lastly for the students of philosophy and religion who ought to know how the most ancient philosophy of the world, the Vedānta, is taught at the present day by the Bhaktas, that is 'the friends and devoted lovers of God,' and continues to exercise its powerful influence, not only on a few philosophers, but on the large masses of what has always been called a country of philosophers. A country permeated by such thoughts as were uttered by *Rāmakṛishna* cannot possibly be looked upon as a country of ignorant idolaters to be converted by the same methods which are applicable to the races of Central Africa.

As the Vedānta forms the background of the sayings of *Rāmakṛishna*, I thought it useful to add a short sketch of some of the most characteristic doctrines of that philosophy. Without it, many readers would hardly be able to understand the ideals of *Rāmakṛishna* and his disciples.

I am quite aware that some of his sayings may sound strange to our ears, nay even offensive. Thus, the conception of the Deity as the Divine Mother is apt to startle us, but we can understand what *Rāmakṛishna* really meant by it, when we read his saying (No. 89):

'Why does the God-lover find such pleasure in addressing the Deity as Mother? Because the child is more free with its mother, and consequently she is dearer to the child than anyone else.'

Sometimes the language which these Hindu devotees use of the Deity must appear to us too familiar, nay even irreverent. They themselves seem to be aware of this and say in excuse:

'A true devotee who has drunk deep of Divine Love is like a veritable drunkard, and, as such, cannot always observe the rules of propriety' (104).

Or again:

'What is the strength of a devotee? He is a child of God, and tears are his greatest strength' (92).

Unless we remember that harem means originally no more than a sacred and guarded place, the following saying will certainly jar on our ears:

'The Knowledge of God may be likened to a man, while the Love of God is like a woman. Knowledge has entry only up to the outer rooms of God, but no one can enter into the inner mysteries of God save a lover, for a woman has access even into the harem of the Almighty' (172).

How deep *Rāmakṛishna* has seen into the mysteries of knowledge and love of God, we see from the next saying: 'Knowledge and love of God are ultimately one and the same. There is no difference between pure knowledge and pure love.'

The following utterances also show the exalted nature of his faith:

'Verily, verily, I say unto you, that he who yearns for God, finds Him' (159).

'He who has faith has all, and he who wants faith wants all' (201).

'So long as one does not become simple like a child, one does not get Divine illumination. Forget all the worldly knowledge that thou hast acquired, and become as ignorant about it as a child, and then thou wilt get the knowledge of the True' (241).

'Where does the strength of an aspirant lie? It is in his tears. As a mother gives her consent to fulfil the desire of her importunately weeping child, so God vouchsafes to his weeping son whatever he is crying for' (306).

'As a lamp does not burn without oil, so a man cannot live without God' (288).

'God is in all men, but all men are not in God: that is the reason why they suffer' (215).

From such sayings we learn that though the real presence of the Divine in nature and in the human soul was nowhere felt so strongly and so universally as in India, and though the fervent love of God, nay the sense of complete absorption in the Godhead, has nowhere found a stronger and more eloquent expression than in the utterances of *Rāmakṛishna*, yet he perfectly knew the barriers that separate divine and human nature.

If we remember that these utterances of *Rāmakṛishna* reveal to us not only his own thoughts, but the faith and hope of millions of human beings, we may indeed feel hopeful about the future of that country. The consciousness of the Divine in man is there, and is shared by all, even by those who seem to worship idols. This constant sense of the presence of God is indeed the common ground on which we may hope that in time not too distant the great temple of the future will be erected, in which Hindus and non-Hindus may join hands and hearts in worshipping the same Supreme Spirit—who is not far from every one of us, for in Him we live and move and have our being.

F.M.M.

IGHTHAM MOTE,

Oct. 18, 1898.

THE MAHĀTMANS

It is not many years since I felt called upon to say a few words on certain religious movements now going on in India, which seemed to me to have been very much misrepresented and misunderstood at home. To people who are unacquainted with the religious state of India, whether modern or ancient, and ignorant of the systems of philosophy prevalent in what has often, and not unjustly, been called a country of philosophers, it is very difficult to understand these movements, more particularly to distinguish between their leaders, who may be open to criticism, and the ideas themselves by which they feel inspired, and which they preach, often with great eloquence, to the multitudes that believe in them and follow them. My article, entitled 'A Real Mahātman,' appeared in the August number, 1896, of the *Nineteenth Century*, and gave rise to a good deal of controversy both in India and in England. My object was twofold: I wished to protest against the wild and overcharged accounts of Saints and Sages living and teaching at present in India which had been published and scattered broadcast in Indian, American, and English papers, and I wished to show at the same time that behind such strange names as Indian Theosophy, and Esoteric Buddhism and all the rest, there was something real, something worth knowing, worth knowing even for us, the students of Plato and Aristotle, Kant and Hegel, in Europe. What happens so often to people whose powers of admiration are in excess of their knowledge and discretion, has happened to the admirers of certain Hindu sages. They thought they had been the first to discover and unearth these Indian Mahātmans, whom they credited not only with a profound knowledge of ancient or even primeval wisdom, but with superhuman powers exhibited generally in the performance of very silly miracles. Not knowing what had long been known to every student of Sanskrit philology, they were carried away by the idea that they had found in India quite a new race of human beings, who had gone through a number of the most fearful ascetic exercises, had retired from the world, and had gained great popularity among low and high by their preachings and teachings, by their abstemious life, by their stirring eloquence, and by the power ascribed to them of working miracles. Mahātman, however, is but one of the many names by which these people have long been known. Mahātman means literally great-souled, then high-minded, noble, and all the rest. It is often used simply as a complimentary term, much as we use reverend or honourable, but it has also been accepted as a technical term, applied to a class of men who in the ancient language of India are well known to us by their name of *Saṃnyāsins*. *Saṃnyāsin* means literally one who has laid down or surrendered everything, that is, one who has abandoned all worldly affections and desires. 'He is to be known as a *Saṃnyāsin*,' we read in the Bhagavad-gîta V. 3, 'who does not hate and does not love anything.'

THE FOUR STAGES OF LIFE

The life of a Brahman was, according to the Laws of Manu, divided into four periods or Äsramas, that of a pupil or Brāhmakārin, that of a householder or Grihastha, of an ascetic or Vānaprastha, and of a hermit or Yati.[1] The first and second stages are clear enough; they represent the scholastic and the married stages of a man's life, the former regulated by the strictest rules as to obedience, chastity, and study, the second devoted to all the duties of a married man, including the duty of performing sacrifices, both public and private. The names of ascetic and hermit for the third and fourth stages are of course approximate renderings only; not having the thing, we have not got the name. But the chief difference between the two seems to be that in the third stage the Brahman still keeps to his dwelling in the forest outside his village, and may even be accompanied there by his wife, see his children, and keep up his sacred fires, performing all the time certain exercises, as enjoined in their sacred books, while in the last stage a man is released from all restrictions, and has to live alone and without any fixed abode.[2] Some translators have used hermit for the third, and ascetic for the fourth stage. In Sanskrit also there exists a variety of names for these two stages, but the distinctive character of each is clear, the third stage representing a mere retreat from the world, the fourth a complete surrender of all worldly interests, a cessation of all duties, a sundering of all the fetters of passion and desire, and a life without a fixed abode. The modern Mahātmans should therefore be considered

1. Manu VI, 87.
2. Äpastamba II, 9, 22, 21, &c.

as belonging partly to the third, partly to the fourth or last stage. They are what we should call friars or itinerant mendicants, for it is their acknowledged privilege to beg and to live on charity.

Another name of these *Saṃnyāsins* was Avadhūta, literally one who has shaken off all attachments, while in the language of the common people they are often called simply Sadhus, or good men.

It has sometimes been denied that there are any *Saṃnyāsins* left in India, and in one sense this is true. The whole scheme of life, with its four stages, as traced in the Laws of Manu, seems to have been at all times more or less of an ideal scheme, a plan of life such as, according to the aspirations of the Brahmans, it ought to be, but as, taking human nature as it is, it could hardly ever have been all over India. Anyhow, at present, though there are men in India who call themselves *Saṃnyāsins*, and are called Sadhus by the people, they are no longer what Manu meant them to be. They no longer pass through the severe discipline of their studentship, they need no longer have fulfilled all the public and private duties of a married householder, nor have remained for a number of years in the seclusion of their forest dwelling. They seem free at any time of their life to throw off all restraints, if need be, their very clothing, and begin to preach and teach whenever and wherever they can find people willing to listen to them.

That the rules laid down in Manu's Law-book had often been broken in early times, we learn from the existence of a whole class of people called Vrātyas. As far back as the Brāhmana period we read of these Vrātyas, outcasts who had not practised brahmakarya, proper studentship[1], but who, if they would only perform certain sacrifices, might be readmitted to all the privileges of the three upper castes. That these Vrātyas were originally non-Aryan people is a mere assertion that has often been repeated, but never been proved. The name was technically applied, during the Brāhmana period, to Aryan people who had belonged to a certain caste, but who had forfeited their caste-

1. Journ. As. Soc. Bombay, XIX, p. 358 (they use silver coins).

privileges by their own neglect of the duties pertaining to the first stage, brahmakarya. There were actually three classes of them, according as the forfeiture affected them personally or dated from their parents or grandparents. All the three classes could be readmitted after performing certain sacrifices. In the modern language vrātyas has come to mean no more than naughty or unmanageable.

It is curious to observe how the Buddhist revolt was mainly based on the argument that if emancipation or spiritual freedom, as enjoyed in the third, and more particularly in the fourth stage, was the highest goal of our life on earth, it was a mistake to wait for it till the very end of life. The Buddhists were in one sense Vrātyas who declined to pass through the long and tedious discipline of a pupil, who considered the performance of the duties of a householder, including marriage and endless sacrifices, not only as unprofitable, but as mischievous. Buddha himself had declared against the penances prescribed for the Brāhmanic ascetic as a hindrance rather than as a help to those who wished for perfect freedom, freedom from all passions and desires, and from the many prejudices of Brahmanic society. It seems almost as if the early Buddhists, by adopting the name of Bhikshu, mendicant, for the members of their order (Sangha), had wished to show that they were all *Saṃnyāsins*, carrying out the old Brahmanic principles to their natural conclusion, though they had renounced at the same time the Vedas, the Laws of tradition, and all Brahmanic sacrifices as mere vanity and vexation of spirit.

Saṃnyāsins or Saints

Similar ideas existed already among the Brahmans, and we meet among them, even before the rise of Buddhism, with men who had shaken off all social fetters who had left their home and family, lived by themselves in forests or in caves, abstained from all material enjoyment, restricted their food and drink to a startling minimum, and often underwent tortures which make us creep when we read of them or see them as represented in pictures and, in modern times, in faithful photographs. Such men were naturally surrounded by a halo of holiness, and they received the little they wanted from those who visited them and who profited by their teaching. Some of these saints, but not many, were scholars, and became teachers of ancient lore. Some, however, and we need not be surprised at it, turned out to be impostors and hypocrites, and brought disgrace on the whole profession. We must not forget that formerly the status of a *Saṃnyāsin* presupposed a very serious discipline during the many years of the student and the domestic life. Such discipline might generally be accepted as a warrant for a well-controlled mind and as security against the propensity to self-indulgence, not quite uncommon even in the lives of so-called Saints. When this security is removed, and when anybody at any time of life may proclaim himself a *Saṃnyāsin*, the temptations even of a Saint are very much increased. But that there were real *Saṃnyāsins*, and that there are even now men who have completely shaken off the fetters of passion, who have disciplined their body and subdued the imaginations of their mind to a perfectly marvellous extent, cannot be doubted. They are often called Yogins, as having exercised Yoga.

Ascetic Exercises of Yoga

Within certain limits Yoga seems to be an excellent discipline, and, in one sense, we ought all to be Yogins. Yoga, as a technical term, means application, concentration, effort; the idea that it meant originally union with the deity has long been given up. This Yoga, however, was soon elaborated into an artificial system, and though supplying the means only that are supposed to be helpful for philosophy, it has been elaborated into a complete system of philosophy, the Yoga philosophy ascribed to *Patañgali*, a variety of Kapila's *Sâmkhya*-philosophy. As described by Svāmin Rāmākrishnānanda in the Brahmavādin, (p. 511 seq.), it consists, as practised at present, of four kinds—Mantra, Laya, *Rāga*, and *Hatha*-yoga. Mantra-yoga consists in repeating a certain word again and again, particularly a word expressive of deity, and concentrating all one's thoughts on it. Laya-yoga is the concentration of all our thoughts on a thing or the idea of a thing, so that we become almost one with it. Here again the ideal image of a god, or names expressive of the Godhead, are the best, as producing absorption in God. Rāga-yoga consists in controlling the breath so as to control the mind. It was observed that when fixing our attention suddenly on anything new we hold our breath, and it was supposed therefore that concentration of the mind would be sure to follow the holding back of the breath, or the *Prānāyama*. *Hatha*-yoga is concerned with the general health of the body, and is supposed to produce concentration by certain portions of the body, by fixing the eyes on one point, particularly the tip of the nose, and similar contrivances. All this is fully described in the Yoga-Sūtras, a work that gives one the impression of being perfectly honest. No doubt it is difficult to believe all the things which the ancient Yogins are credited with, and the achievements of modern Yogins also are often very startling. I confess I find it equally difficult to believe them or not to believe them. We are told by eye-witnesses and trustworthy witnesses that these Yogins go without food for weeks and months, that they can sit unmoved for any length of time, that they feel no pain, that they can mesmerise with their eyes and read people's thoughts. All this I can believe, but if the same authorities tell us that Yogins can see the forms of gods and goddesses moving in the sky, or that the ideal God appears before them, that they hear voïces from the sky, perceive a divine fragrance, and lastly that they have been seen to sit in the air without any support, I must claim the privilege of St. Thomas a little longer, though I am bound to say that the evidence that has come to me in support of the last achievement is most startling.[1]

That what is called a state of Samādhi, or a trance, can be produced by the very means which are employed by the Yogins in India, is, I believe, admitted by medical and psychiatric authorities; and though impostors certainly exist among the Indian Yogins, we should be careful not to treat all these Indian Saints as mere impostors. The temptation, no doubt, is great for people, who are believed to be inspired, to pretend to be what they are believed to be, nay, in the end, not only to pretend, but really to believe what others believe of them. And if they have been brought up in a philosophical atmosphere, or are filled by deep religious feelings, they would very naturally become what the Mahātmans are described to be—men who can pour out their souls in perfervid eloquence and high-flown poetry, or who are able to enter even on subtle discussions of the great problems of philosophy and answer any questions addressed to them.

1. See also H. Walter, Hathayogapradipika, 1893.

Rāmakṛishna

Such a man was Rāmakṛishna, who has lately obtained considerable celebrity both in India and America, where his disciples have been actively engaged in preaching his gospel and winning converts to his doctrines, even among Christian audiences. This may seem very strange, nay, almost incredible to us. But we have only to remember what the religion of large numbers of people consists in who call themselves Christians, without even having had an idea of what Christ really taught or what He was meant for in the history of mankind. There are many who know absolutely nothing either of the history or of the doctrines of Christianity, or if they do, they have simply learnt their catechism by heart. They repeat what they have learnt, but without an atom of real faith or love. Yet every human heart has its religious yearnings, it has a hunger for religion which sooner or later wants to be satisfied. Now the religion taught by the disciples of Rāmakṛishna comes to these hungry souls without any outward authority. So far from being forced on them, it is to them at first a heathen and despised religion. If they listen to it at all, it is of their own free will; and if they believe in any part of it, it is of their own free choice. A chosen religion is always stronger than an inherited religion, and hence we find that converts from one religion to another are generally so zealous for their new faith, while those who never knew what real religion meant are enthusiastic in proclaiming any truths which they seem to have discovered for themselves and to which their heart has yielded a free assent. Hence, though there may be some exaggeration in the number of those who are stated to have become converted to the religion of Rāmakṛishna, and though some who now call themselves converts to the Vedānta may in reality have made but the first step towards real Christianity, there can be no doubt that a religion which can achieve such successes in our time, while it calls itself with perfect truth the oldest religion and philosophy of the world, viz. the Vedānta, the end or highest object of the Veda, deserves our careful attention.[1]

Rāmakṛishna himself never claimed to be the founder of a new religion. He simply preached the old religion of India, which was founded on the Veda, more particularly on the Upanishads, and was systematised later on in the Sūtras of Bādarāyaṇa, and finally developed in the commentaries of Samkara and others. Even in preaching that religion, and in living the life of a recluse, as he did, Rāmakṛishna by no means claimed to stand alone. There were several leading Vedānta preachers in India during the last fifty years, sometimes called Paramahamsas. Keshub Chunder Sen, well known in England and America, who was a great reformer with a strong leaning towards Christianity, was not counted as one of them, because he never passed through the proper discipline and did not live the life of a *Saṃnyāsin*. But he mentions four among his contemporaries who deserved that title: first, Dayananda Sarasvati, for a time unfortunately connected with Madame Blavatsky; secondly, Pawāri Bāba of Ghazipur; thirdly, the Sikh Nagaji of Doomraon; and lastly, our Rāmakṛishna, commonly called the Paramahamsa of Dakshinesvar. 'These,' he adds, 'are the four ascetic saints whom our friends have from time to time duly honoured, and in whose company they have sought the sanctifying influences of character and example. May we respect,' he continues, 'and serve with profound respect and humility, every ascetic saint whom Providence may bring to us. The impure become pure in the company of Sadhus.'

1. This is the explanation given of the name of Vedānta. But it is probably an after-thought. Like other compounds in anta, such as Siddhānta, Sūtrānta, &c., it was probably meant at first for no more than the subject-matter of the Veda; then, as it stands at the end of Brahmanas and Aranyakas, it was explained as end of the Veda, and lastly as the end, i.e. the goal, the highest object of the Veda.

Dayananda Sarasvati

Of the life of the first, of Dayananda Sarasvati, we have very full accounts. He initiated a great reform of Brahmanism, and seems to have been a liberal-minded man, so far as social reforms were concerned. He also was willing to surrender his belief in the divine revelation of the Brahmanas, though he retained it in full strength with regard to the Vedic hymns. He published large commentaries on the Vedas, which show great familiarity with Sanskrit and very wide reading, though at the same time an utter want of critical judgement. He sanctioned the remarriage of widows, supported the movement in favour of raising the marriageable age of boys and girls, and altogether showed himself free from many prejudices as to caste, food, and all the rest. He condemned idolatry and even polytheism. His name became better known in Europe also, from the time that he fell into the net spread for him by Madame Blavatsky. But this lasted for a short time only, and when he perceived what her real objects were, the *Saṃnyāsin* would have nothing more to say to her. She was not quite the Maitreyī he had expected. He did not know English, she did not know Bengali or Sanskrit; hence they did not understand each other at first, while later on, as some people said, they understood each other but too well. However that may be, he certainly seems to have been a powerful disputant, his influence became greater and greater, till at last his opponents, the orthodox and unchanging Brahmans, were suspected of having poisoned their dangerous rival. He died suddenly, but his followers, under the name of Arya-Samaj, form still a very important and growing sect in India, that keeps aloof from all European influences.

Pawāri Bāba

The second Saint was Pawāri Bāba of Ghazipur. Little Is known of him, but his recent death has created a painful sensation all over India. He had lived for about thirty years at Ghazipur, and was venerated as a Saint by the whole native community. The last nine years, however, he had almost entirely withdrawn from the world,[1] living by himself in a compound surrounded by high walls and protected by a formidable gate. Inside there was a small flower-garden, a well, a small temple, and his own dwelling-house, which consisted of one room. He never allowed the gate to be opened, and no one ever saw him except his younger brother. Once every week or ten days, however, he would come up to the gate and converse for a few moments from within with anyone who happened to be there. His younger brother always remained within calling-distance. But though his saintly brother had told him that he could not any longer bear the misery which the Kālī-yuga, i.e. the present age, had brought upon India, he little suspected what his brother meant. The venerable man, after taking his usual bath and performing his devotions, seems to have covered his whole body with clarified butter, to have sprinkled himself all over with incense, then to have set fire to the four corners of his lonely house, and when the flames had taken hold of it on all sides, to have deliberately thrown himself into the fire, thus performing his last sacrifice. Before anybody could rescue him, the old man was burnt to ashes, and what remained of him was consigned with due ceremony to the sacred waters of the Ganges. All this happened only a few months ago. It is always

1. *Interpreter*, June, 1898. *Indian Social Reformer*, June 19, 1898.

difficult to get an exact account of anything that happens in India. The conflagration of the house in which the old Saint had lived for many years cannot be doubted, nor the discovery of his burnt body. But some of his friends, unwilling to admit his self-immolation, ascribe the fire to an accident, while others consider his voluntary sacrifice as the proper ending to his saintly life.

His name Pawāri, sometimes spelt Pahari, is explained as a contraction of Pavanahari, he who lives on air.

His teaching was probably much the same as that of Rāmakṛishna, but I have not been able to get a more accurate account of it. His position, however, as a Sage and a Saint seems to have been generally recognised, and Keshub Chunder Sen is a sufficient authority for the fact that he well deserved a place by the side of such men as Dayananda Sarasvati and Rāmakṛishna. The people of India evidently distinguish clearly between these professed ascetics and saints on one side, and mere reformers such as Rammohun Roy and Keshub Chunder Sen on the other. They evidently want to see a complete surrender of the world and its pleasures, riches, and honours before they quite believe in the truth and the sincerity of any teachers and reformers. Having undergone severe tortures and penances is likewise an essential condition of Sainthood, and for the crowd at large even the power of working miracles is by no means out of fashion yet as a test of being an inspired sage.

The best-known name by which some of these sages are called is Paramahamsa, a name that hardly lends itself to translation in English. Scholars who like to cavil and raise a smile at every custom or tradition of the Hindus, translate it literally by Great Goose, but it would be more faithful to render that ancient title by High-soaring Eagle. Besides, *hamsa*, though it is the same word as goose, is not the same bird. But though these Paramahamsas form an elite by themselves, we know how many men there have been and are even now in India who, by the asceticism and saintliness of their lives, deserve a place very near to the Paramahamsas in our estimation. We know how Udayashankar, the Prime Minister of Bhavnagar, tried hard to revive, in his own case, the strict rules of life prescribed for the ancient *Saṃnyāsins*. The life of Keshub Chunder Sen also, though he was a married man and travelled much and moved in the world, was a life of extreme self-denial, as much as that of any Paramahamsa.

Debendranath Tagore

The same applies to Debendranath Tagore, the friend and constant patron of Keshub Chunder Sen. Though he was the head of a wealthy and influential family, he spent most of his life in retirement from the world, in study, meditation, and contemplation. He has reached now what is considered a very high age in India, eighty-two, and we are glad to hear that he has written an autobiography to be published after his death. As the friend and protector of Keshub Chunder Sen, though for a time separated from him, he has acted a far more important part in the history of the Brāhma-Samāj than is commonly supposed. The following account of a visit lately paid to him by some members of the Brāhma-Samāj will give us an idea of the life of this man. I am in possession of some of his letters, which are very instructive, but which are hardly fit for publication. Some friends who visited him lately give the following account of their interview with the old Saint.

'We were conducted to the spacious verandah on the second story, where the venerable old man was seated on a chair. We bowed down reverentially and took our seats. The Maharshi was the first to speak. He said: "Since you came here three months ago, my communication with the external world has been much diminished. I see things much less and hear much fewer words. But that is no loss to me. As my dealings with the external world are decreasing, my Yoga with the internal world is rapidly increasing. No effort on my part is now required for communion. I sit by myself and enjoy this company." As he spoke these words his countenance glowed with emotion.

On being asked if he remembered the different occasions on which he selected the verses from the Vedantic texts to form the liturgy of the Brāhma-Samāj (published by him many years ago), the Saint replied: "I cannot call back to my mind after such a length of time the process through which these texts were brought together from different Upanishads. I have got the essence of these things within me now, and I am enjoying the sweetness thereof. So there is now no more need for me to go to the texts. I fully agree with you, that from the True and the Intelligent we go to the Infinite person, and that then we find in the infinite splendours and behold his infinite mercy and other attributes. I might have talked much with you on these subjects, had you come a short time before this. Now my mind is mostly occupied with things which the eyes see not nor the ears hear, so I shall not be able to talk much with you. . . . I have written an account of my life as I have been moved by the Spirit of God, but I do not know of what use it will be. Now I have become quite useless to the world. I have now very little to connect me with the world." When we replied that we did not consider his life to have been in vain, as he had given the world an example of a life lived in and with God, the Maharshi continued, "I am living the life of a recluse, I have no energy left. The energy and earnestness you see in me now is roused only by seeing you. Long, long ago, while I was studying the Upanishads, a great light dawned upon my soul and I felt that India would one day worship Brāhmana, the Only True God. I then badly wanted a companion, a man after my own heart, who would have my feelings and join hands with me. I tried almost all the men of light and leading of the time, but could find none. I then left Calcutta in despair and repaired to the hills. After a two years' stay there, the fall of the river Sutlej suggested to my mind a sacred lesson. I heard a voice urging me to go to Calcutta and resume my holy work. I was so much engrossed with this divine voice that nothing would give me rest. Every object seemed to reverberate the Divine injunction and press me to fulfil the Lord's will. In all haste I came back, and as I came back, Brāhmānanda

(Keshub Chunder Sen) made my acquaintance. I saw at once that he was exactly the right man whom I wanted. I could then discern why I was led by the Spirit to come back to Calcutta. My joy knew no bounds. We passed the greater portion of the nights in conversation about deep spiritual matters, even up to two in the morning. Brāhmānanda even told me that when he would be gone, those whom he would leave behind would express and promote my cause. I find his words are going to be fulfilled now." "Yes," we replied, "that is very true. While our minister was with us in the flesh, we did not realise our nearness unto you so much. Our impression is that the Brāhma-Samāj has accepted Raja Rammohun Roy, but has not yet accepted you. As you represent Yoga or direct vision of God, the Brāhma-Samāj will not be able to attain to that feature of spirituality, unless it accepts you. The present deplorable state of the Brāhma-Samāj is owing to its non-acceptance of you." The Maharshi replied: "God has called you to preach the Brāhma Dharma to this poor country of India, and particularly to Bengal—our weak, indigent, and helpless country. As the mother loves her decrepit child more tenderly, so God has shown this greater love to these His poor ones. For this special grace we are peculiarly thankful to God. God has shown special favour to you, and has made you particularly fit for your work. I have published my last work about Paraloka and Mukti, the next world and salvation, in a small volume. I make an offering of it to you." After these words the pilgrims departed, much comforted and helped[1].'

I thought that this glimpse at what passes in India within doors, and is but seldom seen or even suspected by those who tell us so much about the palaces, the Rajahs and Maharajahs, the car of Juggernath, the Towers of Silence, or the Caves of Ellora, was worth preserving and might interest the true friends of India.

We have but to open the Indian papers to meet with notices of men who have led the same saintly and God-devoted life as Debendranath Tagore, but who nevertheless have not reached

1. Unity and the Minister, 1896, July 12.

the rank of a Paramahamsa in the eyes of the people of India. It is quite possible that some of them who are venerated as Saints in their own country, would be disposed of as fools or fanatics by European critics. Still they hold their own place in their own country, and they represent a power which ought not to be entirely neglected by the rulers of 'weak, indigent, helpless Bengal.'

Rai Shaligram Saheb Bahadur

One more case and I have done with my imperfect sketch of the stage on which Rāmakṛishna appears before us to act his part, together with his fellow-actors who supported and often guided him in his unselfish and devoted endeavours. We read in the *Prabuddha Bhārata*, May, 1898, p. 132 seq., of one Rai Shaligram Saheb Bahadur. Saheb Bahadur, who is now about seventy years of age, has spent a very active and useful life as an official in the Post Office, where he rose to be Postmaster-General of the North-Western Provinces. It seems that the horrors of the mutiny in 1857 made a deep impression on his mind. He saw thousands of men, women, and children butchered before his eyes, the rich reduced to poverty, the poor raised to unexpected and undeserved wealth, so that the idea of the world's impermanent and transient nature took complete possession of him and estranged him from all that had formerly enlisted his interest and occupied his energies. From his very youth, however, his mind had been filled with religious and philosophical questions, and he is said to have devoted much time from his youth onward through all the years of his official life to the study of the Sacred Scriptures. No wonder therefore that after witnessing the horrors of the mutiny and its suppression, he should have wished to flee from this den of misery and to get happiness unalloyed and permanent where alone it could be found. He went to consult several *Saṃnyāsins* and Yogins, but they could not help him. At last, one of his colleagues at the Post Office recommended his elder brother as a spiritual guide who could be trusted. For two years he attended his lectures, compared his teaching with that of the Upanishads and other holy writings, and then became his devoted pupil or Chela. During his stay at Agra he allowed no one else to serve his master. He used to grind the flour for him, to cook his meals, and feed him with his own hands. Every morning, he could be seen carrying a pitcher of pure water on his head for the Guru to bathe in, which he fetched from a place two miles distant. His monthly salary also was handed over to the Saint, who used it for the support of his pupils, wife and children, and spent the rest in charity. All his home affairs were superintended by his Guru, and this was done in spite of the opposition of his castemen who were Kayasthas, and did not approve of one of their caste cooking the Saint's food and eating from his dishes, because the Saint was a member of another caste, that of the Khetris. After some time, the pupil wished to retire from the postal service, but the Saint would not allow it. When he was appointed Postmaster-General of the North-West he fell on his knees before the Saint and begged his permission to retire and enter soul and body into the true spiritual life, but the Saint once more refused, saying that the discharge of his official duties would in no way interfere with his spiritual progress. Accordingly, he left Agra, and for many years, held his new post at Allahabad, as it is said, with great success, having introduced many reforms and useful changes in the Postal Department.

It was not till the death of his Guru in 1897 that the Postmaster-General felt himself free and justified in leaving the service. He then became a Guru himself, and imparted spiritual instruction to those who came to seek for his help. Often those who came to listen to him were so inspired by his teaching that they renounced the world and began to lead the life of *Saṃnyāsins*, so that it became a general belief that whoever went to Rai Shaligram would forsake his family and become an ascetic. Nay, it was said that no one could even look at the lamp burning on the upper story of his house without being influenced to renounce the world, to forsake his relations, and thus to become useless to the community at large. When last heard of the old man was still alive, his house was besieged every day by large numbers of persons, both male and female, who flock there from different parts of the country. He holds five meetings day and night for the purpose of imparting religious instruction, so that he has hardly more than two hours left for sleep. Everybody is welcome, and no distinction is made between Brāhmana and Śūdra, rich and poor, good and bad. The people are convinced that he can work miracles, but he himself regards such things as unbecoming, and below his dignity. It is said that the late Doctor Makund Lal, Assistant-Surgeon to the Viceroy, was in the habit of sending to him patients who had made themselves senseless by excessive practice of *Prānāyama*, restraint of the breath, and that by a mere look he brought them back to their senses, and taught them that this practice was of little good, and in many cases injurious.

Rāmakṛishna

The few cases mentioned here may suffice to show that Rāmakṛishna was by no means a solitary instance, and that, however much the old social system of the Four Stages as described by Manu may have changed, there are still *Saṃnyāsins* in India who live the life of the ancient *Saṃnyāsins*, though of course in different surroundings and under different conditions. These cases are as well authenticated as anything that comes to us from India is ever likely to be. If we turned our eyes to the ancient literature of that country, we should see *Saṃnyāsins* in large numbers, but their performances would probably be considered as fabulous, nor should I venture to say that they are what we mean by well-authenticated. The fact, however, that some of these *Saṃnyāsins* reduced themselves by ascetic exercises to mere skeletons[1] or became raving mad-men can hardly be doubted, if we may judge by the warnings against such excesses which appear at a very early time in the ancient literature of the country. A well-known instance is that of Buddha himself, who, before he founded his own religion, went through all the tortures of Brahmanic *ascesis*, but derived so little benefit from them that he denounced the whole system, as then practised, not only as useless but as mischievous, preferring in all things what he called the *via media*.

If now we turn our attention again to the fourth of the Paramahamsas, recognised by Keshub Chunder Sen as pre-eminent among his contemporaries, we shall feel less surprised

1. See a remarkable instance in Mrs. Flora Annie Steel's 'In the Permanent Way,' 1898.

by his life and his doctrines, but accept him as one of a class which has always existed in India. We possess indeed full accounts of his life, but they are often so strangely exaggerated, nay so contradictory, that it seemed almost hopeless to form a correct and true idea of his earthly career and his character. I applied therefore to one of his most eminent pupils, Vivekananda, asking him to write down for me what he could tell of his own knowledge of his venerable teacher, and I received from him a full description of his Master's life. It will be easily seen, however, that even this account is not quite free from traditional elements. If I give it as much as possible unaltered, I have a reason for it.

The Dialogic Process

Such as it is, it will give us an insight into the way in which a new religion, or rather a new sect, springs up and grows. It will place before our eyes the transformation which mere repetition, conversation, or what is called oral tradition will and must produce in the description of the facts as they really happened. We can watch here what is really a kind of Dialectic Process which is at work in all history, both ancient and modern. This Dialectic Process as applied to the facts of history, comprehends all the changes which are inevitably produced by the mere communication and interchange of ideas, by the give and take of dialogue, by the turning of thoughts from one side to the other. It is in reality what is called in German the threshing out of a subject, a kind of *Durchsprechen*, or what the Greeks called a speaking forward and backward, or dialogue. Even Hegel's Dialectic Process, the movement of the idea by itself, that leads irresistibly from positive to negative and to conciliation, has its origin in what I should prefer to call by a wider name the *Dialogic Process*, of the greatest importance in history, both ancient and modern. There is hardly a single fact in history which can escape being modified by this process before it reaches the writer of history. It must be distinguished from the *Mythological Process*, which forms indeed a part of it, but acts under much more special rules. We can watch the Dialogic Process in Modern History also, though we have here reporters, and newspapers, the autobiographies and reminiscences of great statesmen which would seem to render this Dialogic infection impossible or harmless. We can only guess what it must have been in times when neither shorthand nor printing existed, when writing and reading were the privilege of a small class, and when very often two or three generations had passed away before the idea of recording certain facts and certain sayings occurred to a chronicler or a historiographer. It is extraordinary that so many historians should have completely neglected this Dialogic Process through which everything must pass before it reaches even the first recorder, forgetting that it could never have been absent. How many difficulties would have been solved, how many contradictions explained, nay how many miracles would become perfectly natural and intelligible, if historians would only learn this one lesson, that we do not and cannot know of any historical event that has not previously passed through this Dialogic Process.

Let us take so recent an event as the telegram sent from EMS, where I am writing. It was meant to tell the world of the supposed insult which Benedetti had offered to the King of Prussia. That telegram marks one of the most decisive events in modern history, it has really helped to change the whole face of Europe. What do we know of it, even after Bismarck's own confessions, beyond what he thought and spoke in his own mind, beyond what he said to my friend Abeken, who wrote it out and sent it off, beyond what the people in Germany and in France thought of it, said of it, made of it, whether as justifying or condemning the war that sprang out of it. Shall we ever know the *ipsissima verba* of Benedetti, his tone of voice, the tone of voice in the Emperor's reply, the consternation or chuckle when the iron chancellor heard from all parts of Europe the echo of his own words and thoughts. And yet all this happened but yesterday. Benedetti himself has told us what he actually said, what the Emperor replied; Bismarck himself has told us what he meant when he had the cooked telegram published to all the world. Does the historian know then what really happened, what was intended by the words used by Benedetti, by the Emperor, and by Bismarck? Here, in EMS the very spot is shown where the words were spoken, though opinions vary even on this point. We possess now the version given by the French diplomatist which is totally different from that given by Bismarck, and yet they had passed through one Dialogic Process only, that of the old King in his conversation with Benedetti and in his communications with his ministers. Again, every reader of modern history is acquainted with the words put into the mouth of the French officer at Waterloo, *La guarde meurt, mais ne se rend pas*; and every reader of French Memoirs knows by this time the real word which is said to have been uttered at that historical moment. How can we ever hope to escape from the transforming power of oral tradition?

The changes wrought by that power are of course more or less violent according to circumstances; entirely absent, I believe, they never are. And nowhere are they more evident than in the accounts which have reached us of the founding of new religions and of their founders. In the case of Buddhism, it is well known that some excellent scholars have actually denied that there ever was such a person as the young prince of Kapilavāstu, of whose life and doings and sayings we possess fuller accounts than of the founders of any other religion. And let it be remembered that no revealed or miraculous character is claimed for Buddha's biographies, nay that Buddha himself rejected any such exceptional claims for himself and for his apostles, being satisfied with having been a man on earth, which, according to him, is the highest form of being in the world, potentially, and is, even in reality, high above all angels and above all gods (devas), such as they were in his time. Atideva, above all gods, is one of the names assigned to Buddha, showing the estimation in which Buddha and in which the gods were held by their followers.

This inevitable influence of the Dialogic Process in history cannot be recognised too soon. It will remove endless difficulties by which we are ensnared, endless dishonesties in which we have ensnared ourselves. If we once understand that after only one day, one week, or one year, any communication, even a communication given from heaven, must suffer the consequences of this Dialogic Process, must be infected by the breath of human thought and of human weakness, many a self-made difficulty will vanish, many a story distorted by the childish love of the miraculous will regain its true moral character, many a face disguised by a misplaced apotheosis will look upon us again with his truly human, loving, and divine eyes. All honest hearts, whatever religion they may profess, will feel relieved and grateful if they once thoroughly understand the dialectic or dialogic working of oral tradition, particularly where it can be traced back to pure and perfectly natural sources.

It is for this very reason, and because this process can be so seldom watched but can generally be traced in its later results only, that even this slight sketch of what a disciple of Rāmakṛishna, with every wish to be truthful, can tell us of his master, may be of some interest to ourselves both for its own sake and for the light which it throws on the conditions under which every religion has to grow up and to be recorded. Nothing is so human as religion, nothing so much exposed to the frailties inherent in human nature. Whatever the origin of a religion may be supposed to have been, its growth from the very first depends clearly on the recipient soil, that is, on human nature, and to study that human nature as it reacts on religion is one of the most useful lessons of Comparative Theology.

I had made it as clear as possible to Vivekananda that the accounts hitherto published of his Master, however edifying they might be to his followers, would sound perfectly absurd to European students, that stories of miraculous events in childhood, of apparitions of goddesses (Devī) communicating to the *Saṃnyāsin* a knowledge of languages and literatures which, as we know, he never possessed in real life, would simply be thrown away on us poor unbelievers, and that descriptions of miracles performed by the Saint, however well authenticated, "would produce the very opposite effect of what they were intended for. Vivekananda himself is a man who knows England and America well, and perfectly understood what I meant. Yet even his unvarnished description of his Master discloses here and there the clear traces of what I call the Dialogic Process, and the irrepressible miraculizing tendencies of devoted disciples. And I am really glad that it does so, if only it helps to teach us that no historian can ever pretend to do more than to show us what a man or a fact seemed to be to him or to the authorities whom he has to follow, and not what he or it actually was. I have also, as far as I could, consulted another account of the life of Rāmakṛishna published in the late numbers of the Brahmavādin. But I am sorry to say that this account stops with No. 19, and has not been continued.

Rāmakṛishna's Life

Rāmakṛishna, we are told, was born in the village of Kamarpukar, in the Zillah Hugli, situated about four miles to the west of the Jahanabad subdivision, and thirty-two miles south of Burdwan. His life on earth began on the 20th of February, 1833, and ended the 16th of August, 1886, 1 a.m.[1] The village in which he was born was inhabited chiefly by people of the lower castes, mostly blacksmiths, Karmakars, or in familiar abbreviation, Kamars, and hence called Kamarpukar, with some sprinkling of carpenters, cowherds (Gowalas), husbandmen (Kaivartas), and oilmen (Telis). His father was the head of the only Brahmanic family settled in the village. Though very poor, he would rather starve than stray from the strictest path of Brahmanical orthodoxy. The original name given to his child was Gadādhara, a name of Vishnu, which means one who holds the club, and it was given him, we are told, on account of a prophetic dream of his father, to whom, while on a pilgrimage to Gaya, Vishnu appeared, telling him that he, the deity, would be born as his son. It was later in life that he began to be called Rāmakṛishna. We are told, and we could hardly have expected anything else, that his father, whose name was Khudiram Chattopadhyaya, was a great lover of God, a man pure in mind, handsome of figure, straightforward and independent. Rumour says—and what is rumour but another name for the Dialogic Process of which we spoke—that he possessed supernatural powers, particularly what is called Vāksiddhi, power of speech, which means that everything he

1. Even dates are inaccurate in the biographical notices of Ramakrishna, as published in various Indian papers immediately after his death.

told, good or bad, of anybody, would always come to pass. He was highly reverenced by all the people of his village, who stood up whenever they saw him coming, and saluted him, nay who would never talk frivolity in his presence.

It could hardly have been otherwise than that his mother also, Chandramani Devī, was a pattern of simplicity and kindness. We are told that Mathurā Nāth, the rich and devoted disciple of her son, came to her once and pressed her to accept a present of a few thousand rupees, but to his astonishment she declined the offer.

The father proved his independence while still living at Dere, on his own ancestral property. The Zemindar of the village wanted him to appear as a witness on his side, threatening him with confiscation of his property and expulsion from his village, if he refused. Khudiram refused, left his village, and migrated to Kamarpur, a village two or three miles east of Dere. There, through the help of some true friends, he managed to make a poor living, and yet he was always profusely generous to the poor and hospitable to everybody, living chiefly in the company of religious men, performing every kind of worship and trying to realise religion to its fullest extent.

There is a story that Rāmakṛishna's father was going to pay a visit to his daughter one day, some twelve or fourteen miles from the place where he lived. After travelling more than half the way, he came across a Bel-tree, beautifully covered with new-grown green leaves. These leaves are very sacred to a Hindu, and they, use them in worshipping the god *Śiva*. It was spring-time. The Bel-trees were casting off their old leaves, and the man had not recently been able to find any good leaves to offer to *Śiva*. On finding these, he at once climbed up the tree, gathered as many leaves as he could carry, and returned home to worship *Śiva*, without going to see his daughter. He was a great lover of *Rāma*, and his tutelary deity was the pure and divine Sri Ramakandra. He had a little plot of land outside the village, and in the sowing time, after getting a man to plough the field, he would go himself, put a few grains of rice in the name of Raghuvīra on the ground first, and then order the labourers to finish the work. It is said that that little plot of land produced enough, as long as he lived, to maintain the whole of the family. He ever depended upon his Raghuvīra, or the hero of the race of Raghu, the divine *Rāma*, and never cared for the morrow. His son Rāmakṛishna, we are told, had something in him which attracted everybody and made people love him, as if he were of their own kith and kin, even at the first appearance.

The young child used to repeat the whole of the religious operas and dramas, the acting, the music, and everything, after hearing them once. He had a very good musical voice and a taste for music. He was a very good judge of the merits and defects of the statues or images of gods or goddesses, and his judgment was held as final by the old people of the village, even from his childhood. He could draw and make images of gods himself. One of the broken stone images of *Śrī Krishṇa*, which he repaired in later days, is still to be seen in the temple of Dakshinesvara of Rani Rasmoni, about four miles to the north of Calcutta. After hearing a religious drama, e.g. the doings of *Śrī Krishna*, he would gather his playmates, teach them the different parts, and enact it in the fields, under the trees. Sometimes he would build an image of the god *Śiva*, and worship it with his companions. At the age of six, he was well versed in the *Purāṇa*, likewise in the *Ramayana*, the *Mahābhārata*, and the *Srimad Bhagavata*, by hearing them from the *Kathaks*, a class of men who preach and read these Puranas for the enlightenment of the uneducated masses all over India. (His knowledge of the Puranas, the Mahabharata, the Ramayana, and the *Bhāgavata* must have been in Bengali, as he never, according to Mozoomdar, who was his friend, knew a word of Sanskrit.)

The pilgrim road to Puri passes through the outskirts of the village where he lived, and very often a whole host of ascetics and religious men would come and take shelter in the *dharmaśālā* or pilgrim-house, built by the Lahā family, the Zemindar of the village. Rāmakṛishna used to go there very often, talk to them on religious subjects, mark their habits, and hear their tales of travel.

It is the custom in India to gather all the learned pandits or professors of the neighbourhood at a funeral ceremony. In one of these gatherings in the house of the Lahā family, a question arose about some intricate points of theology, and the professors could not come to a conclusion. The boy Rāmakṛishna went to them and decided it quickly with his simple language, and all present were astonished. (This might be taken from any *Evangelium infantiae.*)

Before he reached his teens, he was walking in the fields one day. The sky was very clear and blue, and he saw a flight of white cranes moving along it. The contrast of colours was so very beautiful and dazzling to his imagination, and produced such thoughts in him, that he fell down in a trance. (This would admit of a very natural pathological explanation, and may therefore be perfectly true, though it would easily lend itself to further poetical expansion.)

He was the youngest child of a family of three sons and two daughters. His eldest brother, Ramkumar Chattopadhyaya, was a very learned professor of the old school. He had his own school at Calcutta. At the age of sixteen Rāmakṛishna, having been invested by his own father with the sacred Brahmanic thread, was taken to this school, but what was his disgust to find that after all their high talk on being and non-being, on Brahman and Māyā, on how the soul is liberated by the realisation of Ātman, they would never dream of practising these precepts in their own lives, but run after lust and gold, after name and fame. He told his brother plainly he would never care for that kind of learning, the sole aim of which was to gain a few pieces of silver, or a few maunds of rice and vegetables. He yearned to learn something which would raise him above all these, and give him as a recompense God Himself. From that time he kept aloof from the school.

The temple of the goddess Kālī at Dakshinesvara, about five miles to the north of Calcutta, was established in 1853 A.D. It stands on the side of the Ganges, and is one of the finest temples in India. The temple deeds were drawn in the name of the Guru, or spiritual director of Rani Rasmoni, for she being of a lower caste, none of the higher castes would come to the temple and take food there if she drew the deeds in her own name. The eldest brother of Sri Rāmakṛishna was appointed as a priest to the temple. The two brothers came on the day when the temple was first opened and established, but such were the caste prejudices of Rāmakṛishna at that time that he protested vehemently against his brother's taking service under a Śūdra woman, or one of the lowest caste, and would not take any cooked food in the temple precincts, because it was forbidden in the Sastras. So, amidst all the rejoicings of the day, in which some fifteen to twenty thousand people were sumptuously entertained, he was the only man who kept his fast. At night, he went to the grocer's close by, took a pice-worth of fried paddy, and returned to Calcutta. But after a week his love for his brother made him return again, and at his entreaty he consented to live there, on condition, however, that he should be allowed to cook his own meals by the side of the Ganges, which is the holiest place according to the Hindus. A few months afterwards, his brother became incapable of conducting the services through illness, and requested Rāmakṛishna to take charge of the duties. He consented at last, and became a recognised worshipper of the goddess Kālī.

Sincere as he always was, he could do nothing from mercenary motives, nor did he ever do anything which he did not thoroughly believe. He now began to look upon the image of the goddess Kālī as his mother and the mother of the universe. He believed it to be living and breathing and taking food out of his hand. After the regular forms of worship, he would sit there for hours and hours, singing hymns and talking and praying to her as a child to his mother, till he lost all consciousness of the outward world. Sometimes he would weep for hours and would not be comforted, because he could not see his mother as perfectly as he wished. People became divided in their opinions regarding him. Some held the young priest to be mad, and some took him to be a great lover of God, and all this outward madness as the manifestation of that love. His mother and brothers, thinking that his imagination would calm down when he had a young wife and a family of his own to look after, took him to his native village and married him to the daughter of Rama Chandra Mukhopadhyaya, who was then five years of age, Srimati Saroda Devi or Saradamani Devi by name. It is said when his mother and brothers were looking after a suitable bride for him, he himself told them that the daughter of such and such a man was destined to be joined to him in marriage, and that she was endowed with all the qualities of a goddess or Devī, and they went and found the bride.

He used to hold that some women were born with all the qualities of a Devī, and some with the opposite qualities—the Asurī, or the demoniacal. The former would help their husbands in becoming religious, and would never lead them to lust and sensuality, and he could distinguish them by their mere appearance. A woman, a perfect stranger to him, came to see him once at Dakshi*nes*vara many years afterwards. She was of a noble family, the wife of a gentleman, and mother of five or six children, yet looked still very young and beautiful. Rāmakṛishna told his disciples at once that she had the qualities of a Devi in her, and he would prove it to them. He ordered them to burn some incense before her, and taking some flowers, placed them on her feet and addressed her as 'mother.' And the lady who never knew anything before of meditation, or Samādhi, and had never seen him before, fell into a deep trance with her hands lifted as in the act of blessing. That trance did not leave her for some hours, and he got frightened at the thought that her husband would accuse him of some black magic. He began, therefore, to pray to his mother Kālī (the goddess) to bring her back to her senses. By-and-by she came to herself, and when she opened her eyes, they were quite red, and she looked as if she were quite drunk. Her attendants had to support her while she got into a carriage, then she drove back home. This is one of many instances of the same kind (evidently cases of hypnosis).

Of men, he used to tell the same. In his later days, when crowds of men and boys came to him to learn, he would select and point out some who, he said, would realise religion in this life, and of the rest he would say that they must enjoy life a little longer before they would have a sincere desire for religion. He used to say, 'That man who had been an emperor in his former birth, who had enjoyed the highest pleasures the world can give, and who had seen the vanities of them all, would attain to perfection in this life on earth.'

After his marriage he returned to Calcutta and took upon himself the charges of the temple again, but instead of toning down, his fervour and devotion increased a thousand-fold. His whole soul, as it were, melted into one flood of tears, and he appealed to the goddess to have mercy on him and reveal herself to him. No mother ever shed such burning tears over the deathbed of her only child. Crowds assembled round him and tried to console him, when the blowing of the conch-shells proclaimed the death of another day, and he gave vent to his sorrow, saying, 'Mother, oh my mother, another day has gone, and still I have not found thee.' People thought he was mad, or that he was suffering from some acute pain, for how was it possible for them, devoted as they were to lust and gold, to name and fame, to imagine that a man could love his God or Goddess Mother with as much intensity as they loved their wives and children? The son-in-law of Rani Rasmoni, Babu Mathuranath, who had always had a love for this young Brahman took him to the best physicians in Calcutta to get him cured of his madness. But all their skill was of no avail. Only one physician of Dacca told them that this man was a great Yogin or ascetic, and that all their pharmacopoeia was useless for curing his disease, if indeed it were a disease at all. So his friends gave him up as lost.

Meanwhile, he increased in love and devotion day by day. One day as he was feeling his separation from Devī very keenly, and thinking of putting an end to himself; as he could not bear his loneliness any longer, he lost all outward sensation, and saw his mother (Kālī) in a vision. These visions came to him again and again, and then he became calmer. Sometimes he doubted whether these visions were really true, and then he would say, 'I would believe them true, if such and such a thing happened,' and it would invariably happen, even at the very hour he expected. For instance, he said one day, 'I could believe them true, and not resulting from a disease of my brain, if the two young daughters of Rani Rasmoni, who never once came to this temple, would come under the big banyan-tree this afternoon, and would speak to me,' though he was a perfect stranger to them. And what was his astonishment when he saw them standing under the tree at the exact hour, and calling him by name, and telling him to be consoled, for the Mother Kālī would surely have mercy on him. These ladies of the Zenana had never come to a public place, especially when young, but somehow or other they got a strong desire to see that temple that very day, and they got permission to go there.

These visions grew more and more, and his trances became longer and longer in duration, till everyone saw it was no longer possible for him to perform his daily course of duties. For instance, it is prescribed in the Sastras that a man should put a flower over his own head and think of himself as the very god or goddess he is going to worship, and Rāmakṛishna, as he put the flower, and thought himself as identified with his mother, would get entranced, and would remain in that state for hours. Then again, from time to time, he would entirely lose his own identity, so much so as to appropriate to himself the offerings brought for the goddess. Sometimes forgetting to adorn the image, he would adorn himself with the flowers. Mathuranath at first objected to this, but shortly afterwards, it is said, he saw the body of Rāmakṛishna transfigured into that of the god Siva, and from that day forward he looked upon him as God Himself, and addressed him always as Father whenever he spoke to him. He appointed the nephew of Rāmakṛishna to conduct the regular services, and left him free to do whatever he liked.

The ardent soul of Rāmakṛishna could not remain quiet with these frequent visions, but ran eagerly to attain perfection and realisation of God in all His different aspects. He thus began the twelve years of unheard of tapasya, or ascetic exercises. Looking back to these years of self-torture in his later days, he said, 'that a great religious tornado, as it were, raged within him during these years and made everything topsy-turvy.' He had no idea then that it lasted for so long a time. He never had a wink of sound sleep during these years, could not even doze, but his eyes would always remain open and fixed. He thought sometimes that he was seriously ill, and holding a looking-glass before him, he put his finger within the sockets of the eye, that the lids might close, but they would not. In his despair he cried out, 'Mother, oh! my mother, is this the result of calling upon thee and believing in thee?' And anon a sweet voice would come, and a sweeter smiling face, and said, 'My son! how could you hope to realise the highest truth, if you don't give up the love of your body and of your little self?' 'A torrent of spiritual light,' he said, 'would come then, deluging my mind and urging me forward. I used to tell my mother, "Mother! I could never learn from these erring men; but I will learn from thee, and thee alone," and the same voice would say, "Yea, my son!"' 'I did not once,' he continued, 'look to the preservation of my body. My hair grew till it became matted, and I had no idea of it. My nephew, Hridaya, used to bring me some food daily, and some days succeeded and some days did not succeed in forcing a few mouthfuls down my throat, though I had no idea of it. Sometimes I used to go to the closet of the servants and sweepers and clean it with my own hands, and prayed, "Mother! destroy in me all idea that I am great, and that I am a Brahman, and that they are low and pariahs, for who are they but Thou in so many forms?"'

'Sometimes,' he said, 'I would sit by the Ganges, with some gold and silver coins and a heap of rubbish by my side, and taking some coins in my right hand and a handful of rubbish in the left, I would tell my soul, "My soul! this is what the world calls money, impressed with the queen's face. It has the power of bringing you rice and vegetables, feeding the poor, of building houses, and doing all that the world calls great, but it can never help thee to realise the ever-existent knowledge and bliss, the Brahman. Regard it, therefore, as rubbish." Then mixing the coins and the rubbish in my hands, while repeating all the time, "money is rubbish, money is rubbish," I lost all perception of the differences between the two in my mind, and threw them both into the Ganges. No wonder people took me for mad.' About this time, Mathuranatha, who was very devoted to him, one day put a shawl fringed with gold round him, which cost about ₹ 1,500. At first, he seemed to be pleased with it. But what was the astonishment of Mathuranatha when the next moment Rāmakṛishna threw it on the ground, trampled and spat on it, and began to cleanse the floor of the room with it, saying, 'It increases vanity, but it can never help to realise the ever-existent knowledge and bliss (*Sat-kit-ānanda*), and therefore is no better than a piece of torn rag.'

'About this time,' he said, 'I felt such a burning sensation all over my body; I used to stand in the waters of the Ganges, with my body immersed up to the shoulders and a wet towel over my head all through the day, for it was insufferable. Then a Brahman lady came and cured me of it in three days. She smeared my body with sandalwood paste and put garlands on my neck, and the pain vanished in three days.'

Now this Brahman lady was, we are told, an extraordinary Bengali woman. She was versed in the philosophies and mythologies of India, and could recite book after book from memory. She could hold her ground in argument with the best pandits of the country. Tall and graceful, she combined in herself all the physical and intellectual qualities that would raise any man or woman high above ordinary mortals. She had a fine voice and was well-versed in music. She had given up the world, practised Yoga (ascetics), attained to some wonderful Yogic powers, and was roaming all over India in the red garb of a *Saṃnyāsin*. Nobody knew anything of her birth or family or name even, and nobody could induce her to say anything about them. She was as if some goddess had come to this earth to help men to perfection, moved by the sorrows and sins of this wicked world. She seemed to have known full well that she was destined to help three particular personages, who were very advanced in attaining perfection. Rāmakṛishna had been informed by his divine mother that she would come and teach him the certain way to attain perfection. He recognised her at once, and she recognised him and said, 'I have found out the other two, and have been searching for thee for a long, long time, and to-day I have found thee.' Up to this time, Rāmakṛishna had not found a single soul who could understand his superhuman devotion and perfect purity, and the arrival of this woman was therefore a great relief to him. His devotion and love knew no bounds.

All people were astonished at the wonderful learning of this Brahman lady, but they could not understand how she could sympathise and place even above herself this half-crazed Rāmakṛishna they took him for. To prove that he was not mad, the lady mentioned some *Vaishnava* scriptures, got the manuscripts from some learned pandits, and quoted passage after passage, showing that all these physical manifestations come to an ardent lover of God. It was recorded in these books that all these states, physical and mental, did happen to the great religious reformer of Bengal, Sri Chaitanya, four hundred years back, and the remedies were given, too, by which he overcame them. For instance, this burning sensation, as if all the body were in flames, from which Sri Rāmakṛishna was suffering at the time, was mentioned in these Vaishnava scriptures as having happened to the shepherdess of Braja, to the stainless Śrī Rādhā, the beloved of *Krishna*, centuries before, and again in later times to Sri Chaitanya, when both of them felt deeply the pain of separation from their beloved (God). In both these cases relief came by smearing the body with sandalwood paste and wearing garlands of sweet-scented flowers. The lady held it to be no real disease, but a state of physical disturbance, which would come to all who arrive at that stage of Bhakti, or love of God. She applied the same remedies for three days, and the trouble passed away.

At another time during her stay, he suffered much from an insatiable appetite. However much he might eat, the appetite was there, preying upon him as if he had taken nothing. The Brahman lady assured him that the same had happened to Chaitanya and other Yogins, and ordered all sorts of dishes to be put into his room on every side, day and night. This practice was continued for a few days, and the sight of so much food gradually acted upon the mind, and the false sensation passed away.

The lady lived there for some years, and made her friend practise all the different sorts of Yoga which make a man complete master of his body and mind, render his passions subservient to his reason, and produce a thorough and deep concentration of thought, and, above all, the fearless and unbiased disposition which is essential to everybody who desires to know the truth and the whole truth.

About this time Rāmakṛishna began to practise Yoga, or the physical discipline, which makes the body strong and enduring. He began by regulating his breath and went through the eight-fold methods prescribed by *Patañgali.* His teachers were astonished at the short time in which he came to the realisation and attained the end of all these ascetic practices. One night, when he was practising Yoga, he was very much frightened at two strings of clotted blood coming out of his mouth. The temple services were then in the hands of one of his cousins, Haladhari, a man of great learning and purity and possessed of certain psychical powers, such as Vāk-siddhi, power of speech. A few days before, Rāmakṛishna had offended him by pointing out to him certain defects of his character, so much so that his cousin cursed him and said that blood should come out of his mouth. So Rāmakṛishna was frightened, but a great Yogin who was living there at the time came to his help, and after inquiring into his case assured him that it was very good that the blood had come out that way. It was because he had to teach many men, and to do good to them, that he was not permitted to enter into that Samādhi (trance) from which nobody returns. He explained to him that when a man has attained to the perfection of this Yoga his blood rushes to his brain, and he becomes absorbed in Samādhi, perceives his identity with the Supreme Self, and never returns any more to speak of his religious experiences to others. Only a few returned, namely, those who by the will of God were born to be the great teachers of mankind. In their case, the blood rushes to the brain, and they feel the identity for some time, but after that, the blood flows out again and they are able to teach.

By this time Rāmakṛishna had learnt all that the Brahman lady could teach, but he was still hankering after higher truths, when a Jñānī (a true philosopher) came and initiated him into the truths of the Vedānta. This was a Sanyasin named *Tota-puri*, tall, muscular, and powerful. He had taken the vow of the order from his very boyhood and after a hard struggle, had succeeded in realising the highest truths of the Vedānta. He wore no clothes whatever, and never rested under a roof. When the doors of palaces might have been opened to him if he had only wished, he passed the night always under a tree or the blue canopy of the heavens, even in winter and in the rainy season, never remaining more than three days in any place, and never caring to ask for food from anybody. Free as the wind, he was roaming all over the country, teaching and exhorting wherever he could find a sincere soul, and helping them to attain that perfection which he had himself reached. He was a living illustration of the truth that Vedānta, when properly realised, can become a practical rule of life. On seeing Sri Rāmakṛishna sitting on the border of the Ganges, he at once recognised in him a great Yogin and a perfectly prepared ground for the reception of the seeds of the highest truths of religion. He addressed him at once and said, 'My son! do you want to learn the way to perfect freedom? Come, then, and I will teach it to you.' Rāmakṛishna, who never did anything without first asking his mother (the goddess Kālī), said that he did not know what he should do, but he would go and ask his mother. He came back in a few minutes and told the Saṃnyāsin that he was ready. Tota-puri made him take the vow, and told him how he was to meditate and how to realise unity. After three days of practice he attained to the highest, the Nirvikalpa stage of Samādhi, where there is no longer any perception of the subject or of the object. The Saṃnyāsin was perfectly bewildered at the rapid progress of his protégé, and said, 'My boy! what I realised after forty years of hard struggle, you have arrived at in three days. I dare not call you my disciple; henceforth, I will address you as my friend.' And such was the love of this holy man for Sri Rāmakṛishna that he stayed with him for eleven months, and in his turn learnt many things from his own disciple. There is a story told of the Saṃnyāsin. He always kept a fire and regarded it as very holy. One day as he was sitting by this fire and talking to Sri Rāmakṛishna, a man came and lighted his pipe out of the same fire. The Saṃnyāsin felt enraged at this sacrilege, when a gentle scolding came from his disciple, who said, 'Is this the way that you look upon everything as Brahman? Is not the man himself Brahman as well as the fire? What is high and what is low in the sight of a Jñānī? The Saṃnyāsin was brought to his senses, and said, 'Brother, you are right. From this day forth you shall never find me angry again,' and he kept his word. He could never understand, however, Rāmakṛishna's love for his Mother (the goddess Kālī). He would talk of it as mere superstition, and ridicule it, when Rāmakṛishna made him understand that in the Absolute there is no thou, nor I, nor God, nay, that it is beyond all speech or thought. As long, however, as there is the least grain of relativity left, the Absolute is within thought and speech and within the limits of the mind, which mind is subservient to the universal mind and consciousness; and this omniscient, universal consciousness was to him his mother and God.

After the departure of Tota-puri, Rāmakṛishna himself tried to remain always in union with the absolute Brahman and in the Nirvikalpa state. Looking back to this period of his life in his later days, he said, 'I remained for six months in that state of perfect union which people seldom reach, and if they reach it, they cannot return to their individual consciousness again. Their bodies and minds could never bear it. But this my body is made up of Sattwa particles (pure elements) and can bear much strain. In those days, I was quite unconscious of the outer world. My body would have died for want of nourishment, but for a Sādhu (an advanced religious ascetic) who came at that time and stayed there for three days for my sake. He recognised my state of Samādhi, and took much interest to preserve this body, while I was unconscious of its very existence. He used to bring some food every day, and when all methods failed to restore sensation or consciousness to this body of mine, he would even strike me with a heavy club, so that the pain might bring me back to consciousness. Sometimes he succeeded in awakening a sort of partial consciousness in me, and he would immediately force down one or two mouthfuls of food before I was lost again in deep Samādhi. Some days when he could not produce any response, even after a severe beating, he was very sorrowful.' After six months, the body gave way under these severe irregularities, and Rāmakṛishna was laid up with dysentery. This disease, he said, did much in bringing him back to consciousness, slowly and gently, in a month or two. When the native physicians had cured him, his deep religious zeal took another turn. He began to practise and realise the Vaishnava ideal of love for God. This love, according to the *Vaishnavas*, becomes manifested practically in any one of the following relations—the relation of a servant to his master, of a friend to his friend, of a child to his parents, or vice versa, and a wife to her husband. The highest point of love is reached when the human soul can love his God as a wife loves her husband. The shepherdess of Braja had this sort of love towards the divine Krishna, and there was no thought of any carnal relationship. No man, they say, can understand this love of Śrī Rādhā and *Śrī Krishna* until he is perfectly free from all carnal desires. They even prohibit ordinary men to read the books which treat of this love of Rādhā and Krishna, because they are still under the sway of passion. Rāmakṛishna, in order to realise this love, dressed himself in women's attire for several days, thought of himself as a woman, and at last succeeded in gaining his ideal. He saw the beautiful form of Śrī Krishna in a trance, and was satisfied. After having thus devoted himself to Vaishnavism, he practised in turn many other religions prevalent in India, even Mohammedanism, always arriving at an understanding of their highest purposes in an incredibly short time. Whenever he wished to learn and practise the doctrines of any faith, he always found a good and learned man of that faith coming to him and advising him how to do it. This is one out of many wonderful things that happened in his life. They may be explained as happy coincidences, which is much the same as to say they were wonderful, and cannot be explained. To give another such instance. At the time when he perceived the desire of practising and realising religion, he was sitting one day under the big banyan-tree (called the Pancha-vāṭī, or the place of the five banyans) to the north of the temple. He found the place very secluded and fit for carrying out his religious practices without disturbance. He was thinking of building a little thatched hut in the place, when the tide came up the river and brought along with it all that was necessary to make a little hut—the bamboos, the sticks, the rope and all—and dropped them just a few yards off the place where he was sitting. He took the materials joyfully and with the help of the gardener, built his little hut, where he practised his Yoga.

In his later days he was thinking of practising the tenets of Christianity. He had seen Jesus in a vision, and for three days he could think of nothing and speak of nothing but Jesus and His love. There was this peculiarity in all his visions—that he always saw them outside himself, but when they vanished they seemed to have entered into him. This was true of Rāma, of Śiva, of Kālī, of Krishna, of Jesus, and of every other god or goddess or prophet.

After all these visions and his realisations of different religions he came to the conclusion that all religions are true, though each of them takes account of one aspect only of the

Akhanda Saccidānanda, i.e. the undivided and eternal existence, knowledge, and bliss. Each of these different religions seemed to him a way to arrive at that One.

During all these years he forgot entirely that he had been married, which was not unnatural for one who had lost all idea of the existence even of his own body. The girl had, in the meantime, attained the age of seventeen or eighteen. She had heard rumours that her husband had become mad, and was in deep grief. Then again, she heard that he had become a great religious man. She determined therefore, to find him and to learn her fate from himself. Having obtained permission from her mother, she walked all the way, about thirty or forty miles, to the Dakshinesvara temple. Rāmakṛishna received her very kindly, but told her that the old Rāmakṛishna was dead, and that the new one could never look upon any woman as his wife. He said that even then he saw his mother, the Goddess Kālī, in her, and however much he might try he could never see anything else. He addressed her as his mother, worshipped her with flowers and incense, asked her blessings, as a child does from his mother, and then became lost in a deep trance. The wife, who was fully worthy of such a hero, told him she wanted nothing from him as her husband, but that he would teach her how to realise God, and allow her to remain near him and cook his meals and do what little she could for his health and comfort. From that day forward, she lived within the temple compound, and began to practise whatever her husband taught her. Mathuranatha offered her the sum of ₹ 10,000, but she declined, saying that her husband had attained perfection by renouncing gold and all pleasures, and she did not care for any, as she was determined to follow him. She is living still, revered by all for her purity and strength of character, helping others of her sex to religion and perfection, looking upon her husband as an incarnation of God Himself, and trying to forward the work her husband began.

Though Rāmakṛishna had no proper education, he had such a wonderful memory that he never forgot what he once heard. In his later days he had a desire to hear the *Adhyātma Rāmāyana*, and he requested one of his disciples to read it to him in the original verse. As he was hearing, another of his disciples came and asked him whether he was understanding the original verses. He said he had heard the book before, with an explanation of it, and therefore knew all of it, but he wanted to hear it again because the book was so beautiful, and he repeated at once the purport of some of the verses which followed, and which were about to be read.

He had attained to great Yoga powers, but he never cared to display these marvellous powers to anybody. He told his disciples that all these powers would come to a man as he advanced, but he warned them never to take any heed of the opinions of men. They had not to please men, but to try to attain the highest perfection, that is, unity with Brahman. The power of working miracles was rather a hindrance in the way to perfection, inasmuch as it diverted the attention of man from his highest goal. But persons who went to him have found abundant proofs of his possessing such powers as thought-reading, predicting future events, seeing things at a distance, and healing a disease by simply willing. The one great power of which he made most use, and which was by far the most wonderful, was that he was able to change a man's thoughts by simply touching his body. In some this touch produced immediate Samādhi, in which they saw visions of gods and goddesses, and lost for some hours all sensation of the outward world. In others it produced no outward changes, but they felt that their thoughts had received a new direction and a new impetus, by which they could easily travel in the path of progress in religion. The carnally minded, for instance, would feel that their thoughts never ran after carnal pleasures afterwards, the miser would find that he did not love his gold, and so on.

About that time Mathuranatha and his family went on a pilgrimage, and took Rāmakṛishna with them. They visited all the sacred places of the Hindus as far as Brindabana, and Rāmakṛishna took the opportunity not only of seeing the temples, but of forming acquaintances with all the religious men, and with the *Saṃnyāsins* who were living in these places, such as the famous Tailanga Swamin of Benares and Ganga Mata of Brindabana. These Sadhus assigned to him a very high position, and regarded him not only as a Brāhmajñānī, but as a great religious teacher (Achārya), nay, as an incarnation of God Himself. At Brindabana he was so much struck by the natural scenery and associations of the place, that he nearly made up his mind to reside there forever. But the memory of his old mother made him return home. On his way back he was so much struck by the poverty of a village near Vaidyanath, that he wept bitterly, and would not go from the place without seeing them happy. So Mathuranatha fed the whole village for several days, gave proper clothing and some money to each of the villagers, and departed with Rāmakṛishna contented.

'When the rose is blown, and sheds its fragrance all around, the bees come of themselves. The bees seek the full-blown rose, and not the rose the bees.' This saying of Sri Rāmakṛishna has been verified often and often in his own life. Numbers of earnest men, of all sects and creeds, began to flock to him to receive instruction and to drink the waters of life. From day-dawn to night-fall he had no leisure to eat or drink, so engaged was he in teaching, exhorting, and ministering to the wants of these hungry and thirsty millions. Men possessed of wonderful Yoga powers and great learning came to learn from this illiterate Paramahamsa of Dakshinesvara, and in their turn acknowledged him as their spiritual director (Guru), touched as they were by the wonderful purity, the childlike simplicity, the perfect unselfishness, and by the simple language in which he propounded the highest truths of religion and philosophy. But the people of Calcutta knew him not till Babu Keshub Chunder Son went to him and wrote about him. Rāmakṛishna's interview with Keshub was brought about in this way. It was in the year 1866 that Keshub was leading a life of prayer and seclusion in a garden house at Belgharia, about two miles from the temple of Dakshinesvara. Rāmakṛishna heard of him, and went to see him. Keshub was so much impressed with the simple words, full of the highest knowledge, the wonderful love of God, and the deep trances of Sri Rāmakṛishna, that he began to come often and often to him. He would sit for hours at the feet of Rāmakṛishna and listen with rapture to the wonderful sayings on religion of that wonderful man. From time to time Rāmakṛishna would be lost in a deep Samādhi, and Keshub would gently touch his feet that he might thereby be purified. Sometimes he would invite the Paramahamsa to his house, or would take him in a boat and proceed a few miles up and down the river. He then used to question him on some points of religion to clear away his own doubts. A strong and deep love grew up between the two, and Keshub's whole life became changed, till, a few years later, he proclaimed his views of religion as the New Dispensation, which was nothing but a partial representation of the truths which Rāmakṛishna had taught for a long time.

A brief sketch of the teachings of Rāmakṛishna, and a few of his sayings, which Keshub published, were sufficient to rouse a wide interest in the Paramahamsa, and numbers of highly-educated men of Calcutta and women of noble family began to pour in to receive instruction from this wonderful Yogin. Rāmakṛishna began to teach them and talk to them from morn till evening. At night, too, he had no rest, for some of the more earnest would remain and spend the night with him. He then forgot his sleep, and talked to them incessantly about Bhakti (devotion) or Jñāna (knowledge) and his own experiences, and how he arrived at them. Though this incessant labour began at last to tell upon him, yet he would not rest. In the meanwhile the crowds of men and women began to increase daily, and he went on as before. When pressed to take rest, he would say, 'I would suffer willingly all sorts of bodily pains, and death also, a hundred thousand times, if by so doing I could bring one single soul to freedom and salvation.'

In the beginning of 1885, he suffered from what is known as 'the clergyman's throat,' which by-and-by developed into cancer. He was removed to Calcutta, and the best physicians were engaged, such as Babu Mohindra Lal Sircar, &c., who advised him to keep the strictest silence; but the advice was to no effect. Crowds of men and women gathered wherever he went, and waited patiently to hear a single word from his mouth, and he, out of compassion for them, would not remain silent. Many a time he would be lost in a Samādhi, losing all consciousness of his body and of his disease, and coming back he would talk incessantly as before. Even when the passage of his throat became so constricted that he could not swallow even liquid food, he would never stop his efforts. He was undaunted and remained as cheerful as ever, till on August 16, 1886, at 10 o'clock in the night, he entered into Samādhi, from which he never returned. His disciples took it at first to be an ordinary Samādhi, such as he used to have every day, during which the best doctors even could not find any pulsation or beating of the heart; but, alas, they were mistaken.

Rāmakṛishna felt such an aversion to gold and silver that he could not even touch them, and a simple touch, even when he was asleep, would produce physical contortions. His breath would stop, and his fingers would become contorted and paralysed for a few minutes, even when the metal had been removed. In his later days he could touch no metals, not even iron.

He was a wonderful mixture of God and man. In his ordinary state he would talk of himself as servant of all men and women. He looked upon them all as God. He himself would never be addressed as Guru, or teacher. Never would he claim for himself any high position. He would touch the ground reverently where his disciples had trodden. But every now and then strange fits of God-consciousness came upon him. He then became changed into a different being altogether. He then spoke of himself as being able to do and know everything. He spoke as if he had the power of giving anything to anybody. He would speak of himself as the same soul that had been born before as Rama, as Krishna, as Jesus, or as Buddha, born again as Rāmakṛishna. He told Mathuranatha, long before anybody knew him, that he had many disciples who would come to him shortly, and he knew all of them. He said that he was free from all eternity, and the practices and struggles after religion which he went through were only meant to show the people the way to salvation. He had done all for them alone. He would say he was a Nitya-mukta, or eternally free, and an incarnation of God Himself. 'The fruit of the pumpkin,' he said, 'comes out first, and then the flowers; so it is with the Nitya-muktas, or those who are free from all eternity, but come down for the good of others.'

During the state of Samādhi he was totally unconscious of himself and of the outward world. At one time he fell down upon a piece of live coal during this state. It burned deep into his flesh, but he did not know for hours, and the surgeon had to come in to extract the coal, when he came back to consciousness, and felt the wound.

At another time his foot slipped, and he broke his hand. The surgeon carne and bound it up and advised him not to use it till it was quite cured. But it was impossible. As soon as anybody spoke anything of religion or on God, he went straight into the state of Samādhi, and his hands became straight and stiff, and the injured hand had to be bound up again. This went on for months, and it took six months or more to cure that simple fracture.

Mathuranatha proposed again and again to hand over to him the temple of Dakshinesvara and a property yielding an income of 25,000 Rs. a year, but he declined the proposal, and added that he would have to fly away from the place if Mathuranatha pressed his gift upon him. At another time another gentleman made an offer of some 25,000 Rs. to him, with the same result.

Remarks on Rāmakṛishna's Life

This is all that Vivekananda sent me when I had asked him to write down whatever he could gather from his own memory and from communication with Rāmakṛishna's other disciples. I had warned him repeatedly not to send me mere fables, such as I had read about his Guru in several Indian periodicals, and I believe he fully understood what I meant. Yet we can hardly fail to see the first beginnings of the ravages which the Dialogic Process works even in the first generation. Given his own veneration for his departed master, there is a natural unwillingness, nay, an incapability, to believe or to repeat anything that might place his master in an unfavourable light. Besides, his master was dead when these records were written, and the *de mortuis nihil nisi bonum* is deeply engraved in every human heart. What is believed and told by everybody in a small village, chiefly by his friends and admirers, is not likely to be contradicted; and if once a man is looked upon as different from others, as possessed of superhuman and miraculous powers, everybody has something new to add in confirmation of what everybody is ready to believe, while a doubt or a denial is treated as a sign of unkindness, possibly of envy or malice. The story, for instance, of the Brahman lady who was sent as a messenger and teacher to Rāmakṛishna, will sound to us far from probable. But when I first heard of it, this lady was represented as a kind of goddess who met her pupil in a forest and instructed him, like another Sarasvāti, in all the Vedas, Puranas, and philosophies. The difficulty that had to be solved by this heavenly apparition was, no doubt, the fact that Rāmakṛishna had never received a proper classical education, and yet spoke with authority about the ancient literature and religion of his countrymen. The fact that he was ignorant of Sanskrit, nay, that he did not know a single word of the sacred language of India, is denied by nobody, and has been distinctly asserted by one of his great admirers, the Rev. P. C. Mozoomdar. Of course he knew Bengali, and a man who speaks Bengali can guess the meaning of Sanskrit as an Italian may guess the meaning of Latin. Some of the classical Sanskrit texts exist in Bengali translations, and may have given him all the information which he wanted for his own purposes, to say nothing of his constant intercourse with learned men who would have warned him against mistakes and answered any question he chose to ask. Thus, the *Dea ex machina* was really not wanted. If this Brahman lady was called a goddess, we must remember that Devī is not much more than a title of honour given to high-born and illustrious ladies, nay, that an exceptionally well-informed and enlightened lady might well have been spoken of as an incarnation of the goddess Sarasvāti. In India the distance between deity and humanity is very small; gods are believed to become men, and men gods, without much ado about it.

Mozoomdar's Judgement

Fortunately, in our case we have the testimony not only of Vivekananda, who, as a devoted disciple of Rāmakṛishna, might be suspected of partiality, but we have several independent witnesses, some favourable, others unfavourable. Mozoomdar must be counted as a favourable witness. He stands aloof from the propaganda carried on by Rāmakṛishna's disciples, but he speaks of him in the highest terms. In a letter which he addressed to me in September, 1895, he wrote: 'Both in Keshub's Life and Teachings, and in the old *Theistic Review*, I have frankly and warmly expressed my estimate of that saintly man and our obligations to him. But there was another side of his character, which of course one could not take up, because it was not edifying.' Here we see another ingredient of the Dialogic Process.

Rāmakṛishna's Language

His speech at times was abominably filthy. For all that, he was, as you say, a real Mahātman, and I would not withdraw a single word I wrote in his praise. Rāmakṛishna was not in the least a Vedantist, except that every Hindu unconsciously imbibes from the atmosphere around some amount of Vedantism, which is the philosophical backbone of every national cult. He did not know a word of Sanskrit, and it is doubtful whether he knew enough Bengali. His spiritual wisdom was the result of genius and practical observation.'

There is a ring of truth and impartiality about this, and there is no sign of jealousy, which often breaks out, even in India, among religious reformers and their followers. As to his filthy language, we must be prepared for much plain speaking among Oriental races. In a country where certain classes of men are allowed to walk about in public places stark naked, language too is not likely to veil what with us requires to be veiled. There is, however, a great difference between what is filthy and what is meant to be filthy. I doubt whether the charge of intentional filthiness or obscenity, which has been brought against writers like Zola, could be brought, or has ever been brought, against Rāmakṛishna. It is quite true that Hindus who belong socially to the higher classes, though not necessarily Brahmans by birth, would be more careful in their expressions. We seldom find any blemishes of that kind in the writings of Rammohun Roy, Keshub Chunder Sen, and their friends. But a certain directness of speech which would be most offensive in England is evidently not regarded in that light in India, and every scholar knows that many of their classical poems, nay, even their Sacred Writings, contain passages which simply do not admit of translation into English. In the three centuries (sataka) of Bhartrihari, treating of worldly wisdom, love, and passionlessness, the second, that of love, has generally been left out in English translations. But the spirit of that Srimgara-Sataka is by no means the same as that of Zola's novels. On the contrary, the object of the poet is to warn people against voluptuousness, not as something in itself criminal, which has never been an Indian view, but as a hindrance in obtaining that serenity of mind without which the highest objects of life, dispassionateness, serenity, and clear-sightedness can never be obtained. A most useful edition of all the three Satakas has lately been published by Purohit Gopi Nath, M.A., Bombay, 1896.

It should not be forgotten that in Homer, in Shakespeare, nay, even in the Bible, there are passages against which our modern taste revolts, yet we object to Bowdlerised editions, because the indecencies are never of an intentional character, and would seem to have been so, if they were now removed by us.

Rāmakṛishna's Wife

Another charge which Mozoomdar seems to consider as proved against Rāmakṛishna is what he calls his almost barbarous treatment of his wife. What he means is evidently that he forgot or neglected her till she was seventeen years of age. But this can hardly be called barbarous in India, where it is a recognised custom that a girl of five years of age, as his wife was when he married her, should remain at her parents' house for years before she migrated to the house of her husband and his parents. And that a man in a state such as Rāmakṛishna is described to have been in should decline to live *maritalement*, is again by no means unusual in Eastern, nay, in Western countries also.

Vivekananda told us that when at the age of seventeen his wife went to find him, he received her with real kindness, and that she was quite satisfied to live with him on his own terms, if he would only enlighten her mind and make her to see and to serve God. Such a relationship is by no means without a precedent, and cannot be called barbarous, for *volenti non fit injuria*. Strange to say, I received not many days ago a letter from an American lady who had gone to visit Rāmakṛishna's widow, Mrs. S. C. Ole Bull, the widow of the famous violin player, and deeply interested in the religious movements in India. On July 11, 1898, she writes from Srinagar in Kashmir: 'We were the first foreigners who were allowed to see Sarada-devi, the widow of Rāmakṛishna. She called us her children, and saying that our visit to her was of the Lord, she felt no strangeness in being with us. When asked to define the obedience to a Guru, who in her case was her husband, she replied to the effect that when one had chosen a Guru or teacher, one should listen to and obey all his directions for spiritual advancement, but in things temporal one could most truly serve a Guru by using one's own best discernment, even if at times it were not in agreement with suggestions given.

'When she gladly gave her husband, to whom she had been united by child-marriage, her assent that he should lead a *Saṃnyāsin*'s life, she gained his intimate friendship, and became his disciple, receiving daily instruction. During the years of her life with him she was his adviser, praying earnestly for such purity of motive that she might never fail him. She had also taken the vow of poverty and chastity, and in renouncing the natural joys of a mother, she became with him the spiritual parent of many children.'

It is strange that a man of Mozoomdar's knowledge and experience should have considered the resolve of Rāmakṛishna's wife to live with him as a *Saṃnyāsinī* as barbarous treatment. She herself evidently did not think so, nor have I heard of any other cruelties on the part of her husband. If she was satisfied with her life, who has any right to complain; and is love between husband and wife really impossible without the procreation of children? We must learn to believe in Hindu honesty, however incredulous we might justly be on such matters in our own country. Anyhow, I know of no one else who has taken offence at Rāmakṛishna's spiritual marriage.

Rāmakṛishna's Influence on Keshub Chunder Sen

A more painful misunderstanding has arisen with regard to the exact relationship between Rāmakṛishna and Keshub Chunder Sen. A disciple may mean many things, but Keshub Chunder Sen was never chary in giving credit where credit was due, and he was the last man to withhold the name of master and teacher from Rāmakṛishna or anyone else from whom he had received inspiration, encouragement, or instruction. 'Whoever he may be,' he writes, 'I desire to learn from him. If I see an ordinary minstrel, I love to learn at his feet. If an ascetic comes, I consider that a lac of rupees has come to my house. I learn much by hearing his hymns. . . . I can clearly perceive that whenever a saint takes leave of me he pours into my heart his virtues. To some extent I become like him—*I am a born disciple*.' On the other hand, no one repudiated the title of Master or Guru more emphatically than Rāmakṛishna. A relative of Keshub Chunder Sen, however, who evidently completely misapprehended what was implied by the influence which I said that Rāmakṛishna had exercised on Keshub Chunder Sen, Mozoomdar, and others as his disciples, is very anxious to establish the priority of Keshub Chunder Sen, as if there could be priority in philosophical or religious truth. 'It was Keshub Chunder,' he tells us, 'who brought Rāmakṛishna out of obscurity.' That may be so, but how often have disciples been instrumental in bringing out their master? He then continues to bring charges against Rāmakṛishna, which may be true or not, but have nothing to do with the true relation between Keshub and Rāmakṛishna. If, as we are told, he did not show sufficient moral abhorrence of prostitutes, he does not stand quite alone in this among the founders of religion. If he did not 'honour the principle of teetotalism according to Western notions,' no one, as far as I know, has ever accused him of any excess in drinking. Such bickerings and cavillings would have been most distasteful both to Keshub Chunder Sen and to Rāmakṛishna. Both had no words but words of praise and love for each other, and it was a great pity that their mutual relation should have been treated in a jealous spirit, and thereby totally misrepresented. I can understand that in India, where the relation between Guru and Sishya is a very peculiar and very definite one, one of Keshub Chunder Sen's relatives should have objected to Rāmakṛishna being represented as the Guru of Keshub. Keshub had no real Guru, nor was he a Brahman by birth like Rāmakṛishna. But that he learnt from Rāmakṛishna he, as well as Mozoomdar, has repeatedly admitted. As to myself, I can only say that Keshub Chunder Sen's memory is quite safe in my hands, perhaps safer than in those of his relatives. I stood up for him when his nearest friends forsook him and turned against him. If my words could possibly have been misunderstood in India, I gladly state that neither did Rāmakṛishna act as Guru or Keshub Chunder Sen as Sishya. The only thing that interested me was whether the influence exercised by the former on the latter might possibly account for certain, as yet unexplained, phases in the later spiritual development of Keshub Chunder Sen. It would be a real help in judging of Keshub Chunder Sen if we knew that—to quote the words of Mozoomdar—' his association with Rāmakṛishna developed the conception of the Motherhood of God'; or, again, that 'the strange selectivism of Rāmakṛishna suggested to Keshub's appreciative mind the thought of broadening the spiritual structure of his own movement.' Whether toward the end of his life Keshub became mystic and ecstatic in his utterances, and whether his concept of the Godhead as the Divine Mother was inspired by Rāmakṛishna, I gladly leave to others to decide. By whatever terms these words mystic and ecstatic may be, if translated into

Bengali, in English they mean exactly that spirit which pervades many of the utterances of the so-called New Dispensation, and which was so severely, and far too severely, animadverted on by many of Keshub's European admirers. Mystic has no such terrible meaning in English as its corresponding term seems to have in Bengali. People always seem to imagine that mystic has something to do with mist. Thus, the late B. R. Rajam Iyer wrote in the Prabuddha Bharata, p. 123:

'The Vedānta will certainly be mysticism if it seek to make a man live without food, enable him to preserve his life as long as he pleases, or get stiff like a corpse, dead entirely to the world, though an obscure spark of life may yet linger in the system. The Vedānta will be mysticism if it seek to enable man to work wonderful feats, as flying in the air, leaving the body at will, and wandering in space unobstructed like a ghost, or entering into the bodies of others, and possessing them like spirits, and doing similar things of an unnatural character. The Vedānta will certainly be mysticism if it seek to make a man read the thoughts of others, and lay him in an eternal trance, when he would be more dead than alive, both with reference to himself and to others.' I quote these words partly to show the misapplication of the term mysticism, for all this should not be called mysticism, but fraud and jugglery; and partly to show what the Vedānta is not, and certainly never was, in the eyes of Keshub Chunder Sen or Rāmakṛishna. It was in order to express my conviction that some later phases in Keshub's so-called New Dispensation were not essential to his simple original teaching, that I tried to trace them back to their different sources. If some of Rāmakṛishna's followers have made capital out of these remarks, surely such local jealousies and backbitings may safely be ignored. An honest understanding between East and West, which was one of Keshub's highest ideals, cannot be furthered by the somewhat childish misunderstandings of Keshub's self-constituted advocates. Keshub himself would have been the last person to approve of the spirit that pervades his friend's passionate, though, I trust, well-intentioned advocacy.

VEDĀNTA-PHILOSOPHY

If now we return to Rāmakṛishna, I can assure Keshub's zealous advocate that I never looked upon Rāmakṛishna as the originator of the Vedānta-philosophy. He was not a man possessed of a scholar-like knowledge of the ancient system of the Vedānta-philosophy, nor do I feel certain that even Keshub Chunder Sen had studied Samkara's or Ramanuga's famous commentaries on the Vedānta Sūtras. But both were thoroughly imbued with the spirit of that philosophy, which is, in fact, like the air breathed more or less by every Hindu who cares for philosophy or religion. It is difficult to say whether we should treat the Vedānta as philosophy or religion, the two being really inseparable from the Hindu point of view.

What is curious, however, both in Keshub Chunder Sen's and in Rāmakṛishna's utterances, is the admixture of European ideas. Neither the one nor the other would have spoken as they did, before the English Government began its educational work in India. The bulk of their teaching is, no doubt, Indian to the backbone. It is the old Indian philosophy, properly called Vedānta or the highest goal of the Veda, but there is clearly a sprinkling, and sometimes far more than a mere sprinkling, of European thoughts in Keshub's writings; and we often meet with quite unexpected references to European subjects, not excluding railways and gas, in the sayings of Rāmakṛishna.

It is necessary to explain in a few words the character of that Vedānta-philosophy which is the very marrow running through all the bones of Rāmakṛishna's doctrine. It is by no means easy, however, to give a short abstract of that ancient philosophy, particularly if we consider that it exists now, and seems always to have existed, under three different forms, the Advaita School (non-duality school), the Visishta-advaita School (non-duality school, with a difference), and the Dvaita School (real duality school), the last of which seems hardly to have a right to the name of Vedānta, but nevertheless is so called. The Advaita or non-duality school, chiefly represented by Samkara and his followers, holds that there is and there can be one reality only, whether we call it God, the Infinite or the Absolute, the Unknowable or Brahman, so that it follows by the strictest rules of logic that whatever is or seems to be, can be that one Absolute only, though wrongly conceived, as we are told, by Avidyā or Nescience. The human soul, like everything else, is and can be nothing but Brahman or the Absolute, though for a time misconceived by Avidyā or Nescience. The desire of each individual soul is not, as commonly supposed, an approach to or a union with Brahman, but simply a becoming what it has always been, a recovering and recollection of its true being, a recognition of the full and undivided Brahman as the eternal basis of every apparently individual soul.

The second school, called Visishta-advaita, or Advaita, non-duality, with a difference, was evidently intended for a larger public, for those who could not bring themselves to deny all reality to the phenomenal world, and some individuality likewise to their own souls. It is difficult to say which of the two schools was the more ancient, and I am bound to acknowledge, after Professor Thibaut's luminous exposition, that the Visishtadvaita interpretation seems to me more in keeping with the Sūtras of Bādarāyaṇa. It is true that Ramanuga lived in the twelfth, Samkara in the eighth century, but there were Visishtādvaita expositions and commentaries long before Ramanuga. Considered as a case of philosophical athletics, the rigidly monistic school cannot fail to command our admiration. Samkara makes no concessions of any kind. He begins and never parts with his conviction that whatever is, is one and the same in itself, without variableness or shadow of turning. This, what he calls the Brahman, does not possess any qualities (visesha), not even those of being and thinking, but it is both being and thought. To every attempt to define or qualify Brahman, Samkara has but one answer—No, No! When the question is asked as to the cause of what cannot be denied, namely, the manifold phenomenal world, or the world as reflected in our consciousness, with all its individual subjects, and all its individual objects, all that Samkara condescends to say is that their cause is Avidyā or Nescience. Here lies what strikes a Western mind as the vulnerable point of Samkara's Vedānta-philosophy. We should feel inclined to say that even this Avidyā, which causes the phenomenal world to appear, must itself have some cause and reality, but Samkara does not allow this, and repeats again and again that, as an illusion, Nescience is neither real nor unreal, but is something exactly like our own ignorance when, for instance, we imagine we see a serpent, while what we really see is a rope, and yet we run away from it in all earnestness as if it were a real cobra. This creative Nescience once granted, everything else proceeds smoothly enough. Brahman (or Ātman), as held or as beheld by Avidyā, seems modified into all that is phenomenal. Our instruments of knowledge, whether senses or mind, nay, our whole body, should be considered as impediments or fetters rather, as Upādhis, as they are called, which one feels tempted to translate by impositions. And here the difficulty arises—are these Upādhis, these misleading organs of knowledge, the cause or the result of Avidyā? With us they are clearly the cause of Avidyā; but are they not, like everything that we call created, the result also of that universal beginningless Avidyā, without which Brahman could never have become even phenomenally creative? This is a point that requires further consideration. It is touched upon, but hardly decided, by Samkara in his commentary (pp. 787, 789), where we read:[1] 'The omniscience and omnipotence of the Ātman are hidden by its union with the body, that is, by the union with the body,

1. Deussen, System des Vedānta, p. 115.

senses, Manas (mind), and Buddhi (thought), the objects, and their perception as such.' And here we have the simile: As fire is endowed with burning and light, but both are hidden when fire has retired into the wood or is covered with ashes, in the same manner, through the union of the Self with the Upādhis, such as body, senses, &c., that is, with the Upadhis formed by Avidyā from Namarupa, names and forms, there arises the error of the Ātman not being different from them, and this is what causes the hiding of the omniscience and omnipotence of the Ātman. It is under the influence of that Avidyā that Brahman assumes or receives names and forms (namarupa), which come very near to the Greek λόγοι, or the archetypes of everything. Then follow the material objective elements which constitute animate and inanimate bodies, in fact the whole objective world. But all this is illusive. In reality there are no individual things, no individual souls (givas); they only seem to exist so long as Nescience prevails over Ātman. or Brahman.

Ekam Advitīyam: One without a Second

If you ask, what then is real in all things and in every individual soul? the answer is, Brahman, the One without a Second, the One besides whom there is nothing; but this answer can be understood by those only who know Avidyā, and by knowing it have destroyed it. Others believe that the world is this or that, and that they themselves are this and that. Man thinks that he is an Ego dwelling in the body, seeing and hearing, comprehending and reasoning, reasoning and acting, while with the strict Vedantist the true Self lies deep below the Ego, or the Aham, which belongs to the world of illusion. As an Ego, man has become already an actor and enjoyer, instead of remaining a distant witness of the world. He is then carried along into the Sa*m*sara, the concourse of the world; he becomes the creature or the slave of his accumulated acts (karman), and goes on from change to change, till in the end he discovers the true Brahman which alone really exists, and which as being himself is called Ātman or Self, and at the same time Paramatman, or the Highest, Ātman and Brahman, both being one and the same thing. Good works may be helpful in producing a proper state of mind for receiving this knowledge, but it is by knowledge alone that men can be saved and obtain Mukti, freedom, and not by good works. This salvation or freedom finds expression in the celebrated words Tat tvam asi, thou art that, i.e. thou art not thou, but that, i.e. the only existing Brahman; the Ātman, the Self, and the Brahman are one and the same.

Strange as Samkara's monism may seem to us, yet the current idea that God created the world out of nothing can, strictly speaking, mean nothing else than that nothing can ever exist by the side of God, that God, out of His own energy, supplied both the material and the efficient cause of the world. Ramanuga is less exacting. He is at one with Samkara in admitting that there can be only one thing real, namely Brahman, but he allows what Samkara strenuously denies, that Brahman possesses attributes. His chief attribute, according to Ramanuga, is thought or intelligence, but he is likewise allowed to possess omnipotence, omniscience, love, and other good qualities. He is allowed to possess within himself certain powers (saktis), the seeds of plurality, so that both the material objects of our experience and the individual souls (givas) may be considered as real modifications of the real Brahman, and not merely as phenomena or illusions (māyā). In this modified capacity Brahman is spoken of as Isvara, the Lord, and both the thinking (kit) and the unthinking world (akit) are supposed to constitute his body. He is then called the Antaryāmin, the ruler within, so that both the objects and the souls which he controls are entitled in their individuality to an independent reality, which, as we saw, Samkara boldly denies. Though Ramanuga also would hardly accept our idea of creation, he teaches evolution or a process by which all that existed potentially or in a subtile invisible form in the one Brahman, while in its undeveloped state (pralaya), becomes visible, material, objective, and individual in this phenomenal world. Could our evolutionists have wished for a better ancestor ? Their phraseology may be different, but what is meant is the same. Ramanuga distinguishes between Brahman as a cause and Brahman as an effect, but he teaches at the same time that cause and effect are always the same, though what we call cause undergoes Parināma, i.e. development, in order to become what we call effect. Instead of holding with Samkara that we are deceived about Brahman, that we turn it aside or invert it (vivarta) while under the sway of Nescience, Ramanuga teaches that Brahman really changes, that what is potential in him at first, becomes real and objective at last. Another important difference between the two is that while Samkara's highest goal consists in Brahman recovering itself by knowledge, Ramanuga recognises the merit of good works, and allows a pure soul to rise by successive stages to the world of Brahman, to enjoy there perfect felicity without fear of new births or of further transmigration. With him, as with us, the soul is really supposed to approach the throne of Brahman, to become like Brahman, and participate in all his powers except one, that of creating, that is, sending forth the phenomenal world, governing it, and absorbing it again when the time comes. Thus, not only does Ramanuga, allow individuality to individual souls, but likewise to Iśvara, the Lord, the personal God, while with Samkara a personal god would be as unreal as a personal soul, both becoming real only in their recovered identity. What Ramanuga thus represents as the highest truth and as the highest goal to be reached by a man seeking for salvation, is not altogether rejected by Samkara. It is tolerated, but it is looked upon by him as Lower Knowledge, the personal Brahman as the Lower Brahman. That Brahman is called aparam, lower, and sagunam, qualified, and being a merely personal God, he is often worshipped by Ramanuga and his numerous followers, even under such popular names as Vishnu or Narayana. With Samkara that personal Iśvara or Lord would be conceived as the pratika, the outward face or appearance only, we might almost say as the persona or the πρόσωπον of the Godhead, and his worship (upāsanā), though ignorant, is tolerated and even recommended as practically useful. The Jewish and the Christian idea of God would be in his eyes the same, a pratika or persona of the Godhead. A worship of that God makes the God to be what he is worshipped as (Ved. Sūtra III, 4, 52), and, such as it is, it may lead the pious and virtuous man to eternal happiness. But it is true knowledge alone that can produce eternal salvation, that is, recovered Brahmanhood, and this, even in this life (givan mukti), with freedom from karman (works) and from all further transmigration after death, in fact with freedom from the law of causality. It seems strange that the followers of these two schools of Vedānta have so long lived in peace and harmony together, though differing on what we should consider the most essential points, whether of philosophy or religion. The followers of Samkara do not accuse the followers of Ramanuga of downright error (mithyādarsana), but of Nescience only, or of, humanly speaking, inevitable Avidyā. Even the phenomenal world and the individual souls, though due to Avidyā, are not, as we saw, considered as empty or false; they are phenomenal, but have their reality in Brahman, if only our eyes, by the withdrawal of Avidyā., are opened to see the truth. What is phenomenal is not nothing, but is always the appearance of that which is and remains real, whether we call it the Brahman, the Ātman, the Absolute, the Unknowable, or, in Kantian language, *das Ding an sich*. Besides, it is recognised, even by the strictest monists, that for all practical purposes (vyavahāra) the phenomenal world may be treated as real. It could not even seem to exist (videri) unless it had its real foundation in Brahman. The only riddle that remains is Avidyā or Nescience, often called Māyā or illusion. Samkara himself will not say that it is or that it is not real. All he can say is that it is there, and that it is the aim of the Vedānta-philosophy to annihilate it by Vidya, Nescience by science, proving thereby, it would seem, that Avidyā is not real.

At first sight this Vedānta-philosophy is, no doubt, startling, but after some time one grows so familiar with it and becomes so fond of it that one wonders why it should not have been discovered by the philosophers of any other country. It seems to solve all difficulties but one, to adapt itself to any other philosophy, nay, to every kind of religion which does not intrench itself behind the ramparts of revelation and miracle. The difficulty is to find a natural approach to it from the position which we occupy in looking at philosophical and religious problems. I tried before to open one of its doors by asking the question, what is the cause of all things? and we met with the answer that that cause must be one, without a second, because the very presence of a second would limit and condition that which is to be unlimited and unconditioned. We saw how, in order to explain what cannot be doubted, namely, the constant changes in the world by which we are surrounded, Avidyā or Nescience was called in to explain what cannot be denied—the variety of our sensations. It is curious only that what the Greek philosophers called the logoi, the thoughts or names as archetypes of all phenomenal things, were by the Vedānta treated not as the expressions of Divine Wisdom or of Sophia, but as Nāma-rūpa, names and forms, the result of Nescience or Avidyā. This Greek conception, apparently the very opposite of that of the Vedānta, is nevertheless the same, only looked at from a lower and higher point of view. Nāma-rūpa, names and forms, and Logoi, names and what is named, express the same idea, namely, that as words are thoughts realised, the whole creation is the word or the expression of eternal thoughts, whether of Brahman or of the Godhead, or, in another version, that the world represents the idea in its dialectic progress from mere being to the highest manifestations of thought. That Brahman can easily be proved to have originally meant word, makes the coincidence between Vedānta, Neo-Platonism, and Christian philosophy still more striking, though it would be hazardous to think of any historical connexion between these ancient conceptions of a rational universe. Lest it should be supposed that I had assimilated the Hindu idea of the word, as being with Brahman and becoming the origin of the world, too closely to the Greek conception of the Logos, I subjoin a literal translation of a passage in Samkara's commentary (p. 96, 1). He holds that Brahman is pure intelligence, and when the opponent remarks that intelligence is possible only if there are objects of intelligence, he replies: 'As the sun would shine even if there were no objects to illuminate, Brahman would be intelligence even if there were no objects on which to exercise his intelligence. Such an object, however, exists even before the creation, namely, Nama-rupa, the names and forms, as yet undeveloped, but striving for development (*avyākrite, vyākikīrshite*), that is the words of the Veda living in the mind of the creator even before the creation.'[1] Might not this have been written by Plato himself?

1. See Deussen, Das System des Vedānta, pp. 75, 147.

GNOTHI SEAUTON

We may try now another door for an entrance into the Vedānta-philosophy, which may help in bringing the Vedānta nearer to ourselves, or ourselves nearer to the Vedānta, so that it may be looked upon not simply as a strange and curious system, but as a system of thought with which we can sympathise, nay, which, with certain modifications, we can appropriate for our own purposes.[1]

One of the most ancient commands of Greek philosophy was the famous Gnôthi seautón, know thyself. Here the Hindu philosopher would step in at once and say that this is likewise the very highest object of their own philosophy, only that they express it more fully by Ātmānam ātmanā pasya, See the Self by the Self! But like true philosophers they would let no word pass unchallenged, and would ask at once, who or what is meant by the αὐτός or by the Self? The Vedānta-philosophy has been called a philosophy of negation, which tries to arrive at the truth by a repeated denial of what cannot be the truth. It often defines its own character by Na, na, Not this, not that. First of all then the Vedānta would say, the αὐτός or that which is what we are, the Self; cannot be the body. In the true sense of the word, the body is not, has no right to be called being, sat, because sooner or later it ceases to be, and nothing can ever cease to be, if it really is. As the body is not eternal, it is not real in the highest sense of reality. If therefore we want to know what is truly real, the body (deha or sthūlasarīra) cannot be the αὐτός or the Self.

1. Cf. Deussen, l.c. p. 60 seq.

But if we see that all we know comes to us through the five senses of seeing, hearing, touching, tasting, and smelling, that we cannot go beyond the senses, that we never have nor can have more than sensuous images of the world and of ourselves, and that what we call our knowledge consists in the first instance of these images, not of any realities, which we may postulate, indeed, as underlying these images, but which we can never reach, except by hypothesis, might we not say that our senses as a whole are our αὐτός or Self? The Vedantist would reply again, No, no. Our senses are wonderful indeed, but they are only the instruments of our knowledge, they form part of our body, they perish with the body, and cannot therefore constitute our real Self. Besides the five senses which the Hindus call gnanendriyas, senses of knowledge, they admit five other senses which they call karmendriyas, senses of action, namely, the senses of speaking, grasping, moving, excretion, and procreation. This is an idea peculiar to the Hindus, the former five being intended for action from without to within (upalabdhi), the latter for action from within to without (karman). The images brought to us by the senses, on which we depend for all our knowledge, are what we should call states of consciousness, they are not even our Ego, much less our Self. They come and go, arise and vanish, and cannot therefore be called real or eternal, as little as the body. In all these images we may distinguish the subject or the active element, and the object or the passive element. The passive or objective elements are what we are accustomed to call matter, and this matter, according to the five senses by which it is perceived, is divided into five kinds, viz. ether, corresponding to hearing; light, corresponding to seeing; air, corresponding to touching; water, corresponding to tasting; and earth, corresponding to smelling. This is all that we can legitimately mean by the five elements. They are to us states of consciousness, or vignana only. But though to us elementary matter exists, and can exist as known, or in the form of knowledge only, the Vedānta does not deny its existence, whatever it may say about its reality. If the objects of our sensuous knowledge are all the result of Avidyā, the elements also must share that fate, and cannot claim more than a phenomenal reality.

As, however, there are few, if any, sensations corresponding to one element only, without being mixed up with others, each element is supposed to be five-folded, that is, to contain one preponderating quality, and small portions of the others. This so-called Pankikarana or quintupling is not to be found, however, in the ancient Vedānta; it belongs to the refinements, and not always improvements, of a later age to which we owe such works as the very popular Vedāntasara. A different and, as it would seem, far more primitive conception of the elements is found in the Upanishads, for instance, the Khāndogya Upanishad VI, 2. We generally find in India four elements, or, with the addition of akasa, ether, as the vehicle of sound, five. The most primitive conception of the constituent elements of the world, however, would seem to have been three; namely, what is earthy, what is fiery, and what is watery. These three elements could not possibly be overlooked, and this threefold division is actually found in the Khāndogya, where the three elements are called Anna, Tegas, and Ap, or, as they are arranged there, first, Tegas, including fire, light, and warmth, then Ap, water, and lastly Anna, earth. It is true that Anna means otherwise food, but it can here be taken in the sense of earth only, as supplying food. The first is represented as red, the second as white, the third as black. These three elements also are represented as being mixed in three proportions, and as constituent elements of the human body they are represented as passing through three forms of development, the earthy portion being manifested in faeces, flesh, and Manas, the watery portion in urine, blood, and life, the fiery portion in bones, marrow, and speech. There are many of these purely fanciful speculations to be found in the Upanishads. This, however, should not be allowed to prejudice us against what is simple and primitive and rational in these depositories of ancient thought. But if it is asked, can these passive and active senses be the Self? the Vedantist says again,

No, no; they are not what we are in search of, they cannot be the αὐτός, which must be real, unchanging, and eternal.

If this applies to the ten senses, it applies with equal strength to what is sometimes called the eleventh sense, the Manas, all treated as material, and as products of the earthy element. Manas is etymologically closely connected with *mens* and has therefore been generally translated by *mind*. But though it may be used in that sense in ordinary language, it has a narrower meaning in Sanskrit philosophy. It is meant for the central and combining organ of the senses of perception and action. This Manas performs originally, what we ascribe to the faculty of attention (avadhāna): it acts, as we are told, as a doorkeeper, preventing the impressions of the different senses from rushing in simultaneously, and producing nothing but confusion. It is easy to show that this central sense also falls under the Vedantic No, no. It cannot be the Self, which must be permanent and real; it is an instrument only, and therefore called *antahkarana*—the inner organ. We see here the same confusion which exists elsewhere. There is such an abundance of words expressive of what is going on within us, our *antahkarana*, our mind in its various manifestations, that we are embarrassed rather than helped by this wealth. The worst of it is that as there are so many words, it was supposed at a later time that each must have its own peculiar meaning; and, if it had not, scholastic definition soon came in to assign to each that special meaning which it was to have in future. In the meantime the stream of languages flowed on in complete disregard of such artificial barriers, and with every new philosophy the confusion became greater and greater. It is easy to understand that if each language by itself can seldom give us well-defined terms for the various manifestations of our perceptive and reasoning powers, the confusion becomes still greater when we attempt to render the psychological terms of one by those of another language. For instance, if we translated Ātman, as is mostly done, by soul, we should be rendering what is free from all passions by a word which generally implies the seat of the passions. And if we were to follow the example of others and translate Manas by understanding or *Verstand*, we should render what is meant as chiefly a perceptive and arranging faculty by a name that implies reasoning from the lowest to the highest form. With us *Verstand* is what distinguishes men from animals, while in the Vedānta, Manas is not denied to animals, not even, as it would seem, to plants[1].

It seems better therefore to retain as much as possible the technical terms of Sanskrit philosophy, and to speak of Ātman or the Self instead of soul, of Manas, or possibly mind, instead of understanding or *Verstand*.

We shall see that even in Sanskrit itself the confusion is very great, there being more terms than can be accommodated or be kept distinct one from the other. By the side of the Indriyas, or senses, for instance, we also find Prānas, literally vital spirits, which include the Manas, and as a *conditio sine qua non*, but not as one of the Indriyas, the so-called Mukhya Prāna, the vital breath, that passes from the lungs through the mouth, and which again in a very artificial, if not to say foolish, manner is divided into five varieties. The Manas is then treated, like the senses, as part of the body, being meant at first, I believe, for no more than the central and superintending perceptive organ. But it has many functions, and the names of some of them are interchanged with the names of the Manas itself. We have Buddhi, the general name for perception and mental activity, *K*itta, thought or what is thought, Vignana, discrimination, some of which are sometimes treated as separate faculties. Samkara, however, shows his powerful grasp by comprising all under Manas, so that Manas is sometimes reason, sometimes understanding, or mind or thought. This simplifies his psychology very much, though it may lead to misunderstandings also. Manas gives us the images (Vorstellungen) which consist of the contributions of the different senses; it tells us this is this (niskaya) and fixes it (adhyavasāya). Images are formed into concepts and words

1. Deussen, l.c. p. 158.

(samkalpa); these may be called into question samsaya), and weighed (vikalpa) against each other, so as to give us judgements. Here then we should have in a rough form the elements of our psychology, but it must be confessed that they were never minutely elaborated by the Vedānta philosophers. Even the meanings here assigned to the different psychological terms, were so assigned etymologically rather than from definitions given by Samkara himself. According to him, Manas gives us everything; impressions, images, concepts, and judgements, nay even self-consciousness or Ahamkāra, i.e. the Ego-making, and consequently the distinguishing between subjects and objects, all are Manas. But when we ask, is the Manas, or the Ahamkāra, or Buddhi, or Kitta, are any of the attributes of Manas, such as Kāma, desire, Dhī, fear, Hrī, shame, Dhī, wisdom, Vikikitsā, doubt, Sraddhā, belief, Asraddhā, unbelief, Dhriti, decision, Adhriti, wavering,—are all or any of these the true Self? the Vedantist answers again, No, no; they are temporal, they are composite, they come and they go, they cannot be what we are in search of, the true and eternal Self. It is clear that when we say my body, there are two things presupposed, one thing the body, the other he to whom it belongs. So again when we speak of my senses, my mind, nay of my Ego, we distinguish between a possessor and what for the time being he possesses. But we should never say my Self, because that is tautological: the Self cannot belong to anyone else. If we were to say my Self, we could only mean our Ego, but if we say our Self, i.e. the Self of all, or simply Self, we mean Brahman, Brahman as hidden within us and within the world. At the time of death the organs of knowledge are not supposed to be destroyed absolutely, but while there is another life before us, they are reduced to a seminal or potential form only, and though the outward organs themselves will decay, their potentia or powers remain, dwelling in what is called the Sūkshma-Sarīra, the subtile body, the body that migrates from birth to birth and becomes again and again a Sthūla-Sarīra, a material body. But when real freedom has once been obtained, this Sukshma-Sarira also vanishes and there remains the Ātmān only, or Brahman as he was and always will be. The form assumed by the body in every new existence is determined by the deeds and thoughts during former existences: it is still, so to say, under the law of causality.

Then what remains for the αὐτός, for the Ātmān? The Greek sages have hardly any answer to give; to them the αὐτός, was seldom more than the Ego, Ahamkāra, while with the Vedantist it is distinctly not the Ego as opposed to a Non-Ego, but something beyond, something not touched by the law of causality, something neither suffering, nor enjoying, nor acting, but that without which neither the gross nor the subtile body could ever exist. This Self, this the true αὐτός, was discovered in the lotus of the heart in true Self-consciousness, it was discovered as not-personal; though dwelling in the personal or living Ātmān, the Giva, it remained forever a mere looker-on, untouched by anything. As I said before, the Vedānta-philosophy is a philosophy of negation; it says No, no, it says all that the Self is not, but what the Self is, defies all words and all thoughts. Our thoughts and our words return from it baffled, as the Veda says. There are passages in the Upanishads where attempts are made to bring us nearer to a conception of the Self, whether we call it the Brahman or the Ātman, but these attempts never go so far as a definition of these two, or of this One Power. In the Khāndogya Upanishad III, 14, we read: 'Surely this universe is Brahman. It should be worshipped in silence as the beginning, the being, and the end of all. Its matter is thought, life its body, light its form. Its will is truth, its Self the infinite (ether). It works all, it wills all, it scents all, it tastes all, embracing the Universe, silent and unconcerned. This is the Self in the innermost heart, smaller than a mustard-seed or the kernel of it. This is the Self in the innermost heart, larger than the earth, larger than the atmosphere, larger than the sky, larger than all worlds. The all-working, all-willing, all-scenting, all-tasting one, the all-embracing, silent, unconcerned one, this is the Self in the innermost heart, this is Brahman, this I shall become when parting from hence. He who has this, does not doubt.

This subject is treated again and again. Very much as we saw it treated in the Khāndogya, we find it treated in the Taittiriya Upanishad II, 1-7. One covering after another is there removed, till there remains in the end the pure Self. First the body of flesh and blood is re-moved, then the vital breath, then the Manas, and with it thought, till at last nothing remains but the Self full of bliss. This is called the sap or the essence. It is this Self that brings bliss, finding peace and rest in the invisible, the immaterial, the inexpressible, the unfathomable. So long as anything else is left, hidden anywhere, there is no peace and no rest, however wise a man may think himself. Or, as Yāgñavalkya says: 'He who knows this, knows everything.' Every name that can be imagined for expressing what is really inexpressible, is assigned in the Upanishads to Brahman. Brahman is neither long nor short, neither subtile nor gross; he is without parts, without activity, still, without spot, without fraud, he is unborn, never growing old, not fading nor dying, nor fearing anything; he is without and within.' Whether such a being can be called he, is very doubtful, for he is neither he nor she; he is It in the very highest sense of that undifferentiated pronoun.

We thus see that both methods, the first that started from the postulate that the true Self must be one, without a second, and the second, which holds that the true Self must be unchanging, eternal, without beginning or end, arrive at the same final result, viz. that the Self of the world can be nothing that is perceived in this changing world, and that our own Self too can be nothing that is perceived as changing, as being born, as living and dying. Both may, in one sense of the word, be called nothings; though they are in reality that in comparison with which everything else is nothing. If the world is real the Self is not, if the Self is real the world is not.

Final Conclusion, Tat tvamasi

Then follows the final conclusion that these two Selfs are one and the same, only reached by different methods. Man is man phenomenally, the world is world phenomenally, the gods of the world are gods phenomenally, but in full reality all are the Godhead, call it Ātman or Brahman, metamorphosed and hidden for a time by Avidyā or Nescience, but always recoverable by Vidya or by the Vedānta-philosophy.

These ideas in a more or less popular form seem to pervade the Hindu mind from the earliest to the latest date. They are taught in the schools, but even without the schools they seem to be imbibed with the mother's milk. They are often exaggerated and caricatured so as to become repulsive to a European mind, but in their purity and simplicity they contain an amount of truth which can no longer be safely neglected by any student, whether of philosophy or religion. It can no longer be put aside as merely curious, or disposed of as mystic, without a definition of what is meant by mystic, and without an argument that everything that is called mystic has really nothing to do with either religion or philosophy. That it may lead to dangerous consequences no one would deny, but the same may be said of almost every religion and every philosophy, if carried to its last consequences. I have already drawn attention to the false reasoning, that because good works cannot secure salvation, therefore bad works also are indifferent or harmless. Good works, according to the Vedānta, certainly do not lead straight to salvation, but they represent the first essential step that leads on to salvation, while evil deeds form a barrier that keeps a man from making even the first step in his progress towards knowledge and beatitude. That a Saint cannot sin, or that *Sciens non peccat*, has been held true not in India only, but it is easily seen in what sense this is either true or false, whether in India or at home. It cannot be deeply enough impressed on the minds of the modern apostles of Rāmakṛishna that nothing would be more likely to lower their master and their own work in the eyes of serious people than the slightest moral laxity on their part, or a defence of any such laxity on the ground that a Gnanin, a Knower, is above morality. It is one thing to say that such a man cannot sin because his passions are completely subdued, another that if he should from any defect of knowledge lapse from his passionless and perfect state it could not be imputed to him as sin. I confess there is a little uncertainty on that point even among ancient authorities, but we know as yet far too little of the classical Vedantic writings to speak with confidence on such a point. There are too many passages in which strict morality is enjoined as a *sine qua non* for Vedantic freedom to allow anyone to use a few doubtful passages in defence of immorality. When we have first learnt all that can be learnt from the Vedānta, it will be time to begin to criticise it, or, if possible, to improve it. We study the systems of Plato and Aristotle, of Spinoza and Kant, not as containing the full and perfect truth, cut and dry, but as helping us on towards the truth. Everyone of these contains partial truths which might easily be proved to lead to dangerous consequences. What is necessary to us at present, more than at any previous time, is a historical study of all philosophy, that of India not excluded, in its genetic or dialectic development, so that we may not be swayed by every philosophical breeze that announces itself as new, though it has been discussed again and again before, and, it may be, far more thoroughly than by its most recent advocates. It will hereafter sound almost incredible that in our time the philosophical public should have been startled by the idea of evolution as a philosophical novelty, nay, that there should have been an angry contest as to who was really the first discoverer of what has been discussed again and again during the last two thousand years. What is parināma, if not evolution, the evolution advocated by Ramanuga, but rejected by Samkara. That the illustration of this evolutionary process of the world, as given in our time, should stand incomparably higher than anything attempted from Ramanuga down to Herder, who would deny? But to the historian of philosophy the idea is one thing, its illustration of it quite another. It is most unfair to represent a man like Darwin, who was the most eminent observer of nature, as a philosopher, an abstract philosopher; the very thing which he himself would have most strongly deprecated.

At present, however, I am not concerned with Indian philosophy, *pure et simple*, but with its effects on the popular mind of India, as shown by one of its recent representatives, Rāmakṛishna. He himself distinguishes very clearly between philosophy or Jñāna (knowledge) and devotion or Bhakti, and he himself was a Bhakta, a worshipper[1] or lover of the deity, much more than a Jñānin or a knower. It was in order to show the background from which Rāmakṛishna emerges, and the lights and shades of the atmosphere in which he moved, that I thought it useful to add a short sketch of Vedantic thought. Rāmakṛishna was in no sense of the word an original thinker, the discoverer of a new idea or the propounder of any new view of the world. But he saw many things which others had not seen, he recognised the Divine Presence where it was least suspected, he was a poet, an enthusiast, or, if you like, a dreamer of dreams. But such dreams also have a right to exist, and have a claim on our attention and sympathy. Rāmakṛishna never composed a philosophical treatise; he simply poured out short sayings, and the people came to listen

1. This difference between Bhakti, devotion, and Jñāna, knowledge, is fully treated by Kishori Lal Sarkar in his interesting little book, The Hindu System of Religious Science and Art, or the Revelations of Rationalism and Emotionalism, Calcutta, 1898. 'Jñāna, the author says, 'sees with a telescopic, Bhakti with a microscopic eye. Jñāna perceives the essence, Bhakti feels the sweetness. Jñāna discovers the Supreme Intelligence, Bhakti reciprocates the Supreme Loving Will'.

to them, whether the speaker was at the time in full possession of his faculties, or in a dream, or in a trance. From all we can learn, it is quite clear that he had, by a powerful control of his breath, and by long continued ascetic exercises, arrived at such a pitch of nervous excitability that he could at any moment faint away or fall into a state of unconsciousness, the so-called Samādhi. This Samādhi may be looked at, however, from two points, as either purely physical or as psychical. From an ordinary Samādhi a man may recover as one recovers from a fainting fit, but the true Samādhi consists in losing oneself or finding oneself entirely in the Supreme Spirit. From this Samādhi there is no return, because there is nothing left that can return. A few men only who have reached it, are enabled to return from it by means of a small remnant of their Ego, and through the efficacy of their wish to become the instructors and saviours of mankind. Something very like Samādhi is the state of deep dreamless sleep, during which the soul is supposed to be with Brahman for a time, but able to return. This deep, unconscious sleep is one of the four states, waking, sleeping with dreams, sleeping without dreams, and dying. With Rāmakṛishna it often happened that when he had fallen into this deep sleep, he remained in it so long that his friends were afraid he would never return to consciousness, and so it was at last at the time of his death. He had fallen into a trance, and he never awoke, but even death could lay hold of his body and his breath only; his Self, no longer his, had recovered its Brahmahood, had become what it had always been and always will be, the Ātman, the Highest Self, in all its glory, freed from all the clouds of appearances, and independent of individuality, personality, and of the whole phenomenal world.

The Sayings of Rāmakṛishna

His sayings or Logia were collected and written down by his pupils, in Bengali; some were translated into Sanskrit and into English. There are many that remind us of old Sanskrit sayings, of which there are several collections, all, however, in metrical form. The sayings of Rāmakṛishna are different, because they are in prose, uttered evidently on the spur of the moment, and tinged here and there with European ideas which must have reached Rāmakṛishna through his intercourse with Anglo-Indians, and not from books, for he was ignorant of English. I received a complete collection of them from Rāmakṛishna's own pupil, Vivekananda, well known by his missionary labours in the United States and England. I give them as they were sent to me, with such corrections only as seemed absolutely necessary. I thought at first of arranging them under different heads, but found that this would have destroyed their character and made them rather monotonous reading. I believe as they are, they give a true picture of the man and of his way of teaching, suggested by the impulses of the moment, but by no means systematic, and by no means free from repetitions and contradictions. I should have liked very much to leave out some of his sayings, because, to our mind, they seem insipid, in bad taste, or even blasphemous. But should I not in doing so have offended against historic truth? We want to know the man who has exercised and is exercising so wide an influence, such as he was, not such as we wish him to have been. He himself never wished to appear different from what he was, and he often seems to have made himself out worse than he was. Besides, if I had done so, I know that there are men who would not have been ashamed of suspecting me of a wish to represent the religions of the East, both modern and ancient, as better than they really are. These are the very men who would find many a lesson to learn from Rāmakṛishna's sayings. No, I said, let the wheat and the tares remain together. Few thoughtful readers will go through them without finding some thought that makes them ponder, some truth that will startle them as coming from so unexpected a quarter. Nothing, on the other hand, would be easier than to pick out a saying here and there, and thus to show that they are all insipid and foolish. This is a very old trick, described in India as the trick of the rice-merchants who wish to sell or to buy a rice-field, and who offer you a handful of good or bad grains to show that the field is either valuable or worthless. To my mind these sayings, the good, the bad, and the indifferent, are interesting because they represent an important phase of thought, an attempt to give prominence to the devotional and practical side of the Vedānta, and because they show the compatibility of the Vedānta with other religions. They will make it clear that the Vedānta also possesses a morality of its own, which may seem too high and too spiritual for ordinary mortals, but which in India has done good, is doing good, and may continue to do good for centuries to come.

In conclusion, I have to thank my friend Mozoomdar, and several of the disciples of Rāmakṛishna, more particularly Vivekananda and the editor of the Brahmavadin, for the ready help they have rendered me in publishing this collection of the sayings of their departed Master.

The Sayings of Rāmakṛishna[1]

1. Thou seest many stars at night in the sky, but findest them not when the sun rises. Canst thou say that there are no stars, then, in the heaven of day? So, O man, because thou beholdest not the Almighty in the days of thy ignorance, say not that there is no God.
2. As one and the same material, viz. water, is called by different names by different people—one calling it 'water,' another 'vari,' a third 'aqua,' and another 'pani'—so the one Sat-*k*it-ānanda, the Everlasting-Intelligent-Bliss, is invoked by some as God, by some as Allah, by some as Hari, and by others as Brahman.
3. Two persons were hotly disputing as to the colour of a chameleon. One said, 'The chameleon on that palm-tree is of a beautiful red colour.' The other, contradicting him, said, 'You are mistaken, the chameleon is not red, but blue.' Not being able to settle the matter by arguments, both went to the person who always lived under that tree and had watched the chameleon in all its phases of colour. One of them said, 'Sir, is not the chameleon on that tree of a red colour?' The person replied, 'Yes, sir.' The other disputant said, 'What do you say? How is it? It is not red, it is blue.' That person again humbly replied, 'Yes, sir.' The person knew that the chameleon is

1. Some more of Ramakrishna's sayings have been sent to me lately, but their publication will have to wait for another opportunity

an animal that constantly changes its colour; thus, it was that he said 'yes' to both these conflicting statements. The Sat-*k*it-ānanda likewise has various forms. The devotee who has seen God in one aspect only, knows Him in that aspect alone. But he who has seen Him in His manifold aspects, is alone in a position to say, 'All these forms are of one God, for God is multiform.' He has forms and has no forms, and many are His forms which no one knows.

4. Many are the names of God, and infinite the forms that lead us to know Him. In whatsoever name or form you desire to call Him, in that very form and name you will see Him.

5. Four blind men went to see an elephant. One touched the leg of the elephant, and said, 'The elephant is like a pillar.' The second touched the trunk, and said, 'The elephant is like a thick stick or club.' The third touched the belly, and said, 'The elephant is like a big jar.' The fourth touched the ears, and said, 'The elephant is like a winnowing basket.' Thus, they began to dispute amongst themselves as to the figure of the elephant. A passer-by seeing them thus quarrelling, said, 'What is it that you are disputing about?' They told him everything, and asked him to arbitrate. That man said, 'None of you has seen the elephant. The elephant is not like a pillar, its legs are like pillars. It is not like a big water-vessel, its belly is like a water-vessel. It is not like a winnowing basket, its ears are like winnowing baskets. It is not like a thick stick or club, but its proboscis is like that. The elephant is the combination of all these.' In the same manner those quarrel who have seen one aspect only of the Deity.

6. As the same sugar is made into various figures of birds and beasts, so one sweet Mother Divine is worshipped in various climes and ages under various names and forms. Different creeds are but different paths to reach the Almighty.

7. As with one gold various ornaments are made, having different forms and names, so one God is worshipped in different countries and ages, and has different forms and names. Though He may be worshipped variously, some loving to call him Father, others Mother, &c., yet it is one God that is being worshipped in all these various relations and modes.

8. *Q.* If the God of every religion is the same, why is it then that the God is painted differently by different religionists?
   A. God is one, but His aspects are different: as one master of the house is father to one, brother to another, and husband to a third, and is called by these different names by those different persons, so one God is described and called in various ways according to the particular aspect in which He appears to His particular worshipper.

9. In a potter's shop there are vessels of different shapes and forms—pots, jars, dishes, plates, &c.—but all are made of one clay. So God is one, but is worshipped in different ages and climes under different names and aspects.

10. God is one, but his aspects are many. One and the same fish may be made to taste differently, according to the different modes of preparing it, so one God is enjoyed variously (i.e. in His various aspects) by His devotees.

11. Man is like a pillow-case. The colour of one may be red, another blue, another black, but all contain the same cotton So it is with man—one is beautiful, one is black, another is holy, a fourth wicked; but the Divine dwells in them all.

12. All waters are brooded over by Narayana, but every kind of water is not fit for drink. Similarly, though it is true that the Almighty dwells in every place, yet every place is not fit to be visited by man. As one kind of water may be used for washing our feet, another may serve the purpose of ablution, and others may be drunk, and others again may

not be touched at all; so there are different kinds of places. We may approach some, we can enter into the inside of others, others we must avoid, even at a distance.

13. It is true that God is even in the tiger, but we must not go and face the animal. So it is true that God dwells even in the most wicked, but it is not meet that we should associate with the wicked.

14. The manifestation of the Divinity must be under-stood to be in greater degree in those who are honoured, respected, and obeyed by a large following, than in those who have gained no such influence.

15. The Master said: 'Everything that exists is God.' The pupil understood it literally, but not in the true spirit. While he was passing through a street, he met with an elephant. The driver (mahut) shouted aloud from his high place, 'Move away, move away!' The pupil argued in his mind, 'Why should I move away? I am God, so is the elephant also God. What fear has God of Himself?' Thinking thus he did not move. At last the elephant took him up by his trunk, and dashed him aside. He was severely hurt, and going back to his Master, he related the whole adventure. The Master said, 'All right, you are God. The elephant is God also, but God in the shape of the elephant-driver was warning you also from above. Why did you not pay heed to his warnings?'

16. God, His scripture (the Bhagavata), and His devotee are all to be regarded as one, i.e. in one and the same light.

17. Every being is Narayana. Man or animal, sage or knave, nay, the whole universe, is Narayana, the Supreme Spirit.

18. As many have merely heard of snow but not seen it, so many are the religious preachers who have read only in books about the attributes of God, but have not realised them in their lives. And as many may have seen but not tasted it, so many are the religious teachers who have got

only a glimpse of Divine Glory, but have not understood its real essence. He who has tasted the snow can say what it is like. He who has enjoyed the society of God in different aspects, now as a servant, now as a friend, now as a lover, or as being absorbed in Him, &c., he alone can tell what are the attributes of God.

19. As the lamp does not burn without oil, so man cannot live without God.

20. The human body is like a boiling pot, and the mind and the senses are like water, rice or potato, &c. in it. Put the pot with its ingredients on the fire; it will be so hot as to burn your finger when you touch it. But the heat does not belong to the pot, nor anything contained in it, but is in the fire. So, it is the fire of Brahman in man that causes the mind and the senses to perform their functions, and when that fire ceases to act, the senses also, or the organs, stop.

21. Says God, 'I am the snake that biteth and the charmer that healeth; I am the judge that condemneth and the executioner that whippeth.'

22. God tells the thief to go and steal, and at the same time warns the householder against the thief.

23. How doth the Lord dwell in the body? He dwells in the body like the plug of a syringe, i.e. in the body, and yet apart from it.

24. The Lord can pass an elephant through the eye of a needle. He can do whatever He likes.

25. As fishes playing in a pond covered over with reeds and scum cannot be seen from outside, so God plays in the heart of a man invisibly, being screened by Māyā from human view.

26. A man sitting under the shade of the Kalpa-vriksha (wishing-tree) wished to be a king, and in an instant

he was a king. The next moment he wished to have a charming damsel, and the damsel was instantly by his side. The man then thought within himself, if a tiger came and devoured him, and alas! in an instant he was in the jaws of a tiger! God is like that wishing-tree: whosoever in His presence thinks that he is destitute and poor, remains as such, but he who thinks and believes that the Lord fulfils all his wants, receives everything from Him.

27. The landlord may be very rich, but when a poor cultivator brings a humble present to him with a loving heart, he accepts it with the greatest pleasure and satisfaction.

28. While a bell is being rung, the repeated ding-dongs can be distinguished one from the other, but when we stop ringing, then an undistinguishable sound only remains audible. We can easily distinguish one note from the other, as if each distinct note had a certain shape; but the continued and unbroken sound when the ding-dongs have ceased is undistinguishable, as if formless. Like the sound of the bell, God is both with and without form.

29. As a boy begins to learn writing by drawing big scrawls, before he can master the small-hand, so we must learn concentration of the mind by fixing it first on forms; and when we have attained success therein, we can easily fix it upon the formless.

30. As a marksman learns to shoot by first taking aim at large and big objects, and the more he acquires the facility, the greater becomes the ease with which he can shoot at the smaller marks on the target, so when the mind has been trained to be fixed on images having form, it becomes easy for it to be fixed upon images having no form.

31. God is the Absolute and Eternal Brahman, as well as the Father of the Universe. The indivisible Brahman is like a vast shoreless ocean, without bounds and limits, in which I can only struggle and sink. But when I approach the

always sportive (active) personal Deity (Hari), I get peace, like the sinking man who nears the shore.

32. God is formless, and is with form too, and He is that which transcends both form and formlessness. He alone can say what else He is.

33. At a certain stage of his path of devotion, the devotee finds satisfaction in God with form; at another stage, in God without form.

34. The God with form is visible, nay, we can touch Him face to face, as with one's dearest friend.

35. As at one time I am clothed, and at another time naked, so Brahman is at one time with attributes and at another without.

36. As water when congealed becomes ice, so the visible form of the Almighty is the materialised manifestation of the all-pervading formless Brahman. It may be called, in fact, Sat-*k*it-ānanda solidified. As the ice, being part and parcel of the water, remains in the water for a time and afterwards melts in it, so the Personal God is part and parcel of the Impersonal. He rises from the Impersonal, remains there, and ultimately merges into it and disappears.

37. His name is Intelligence; His abode is Intelligence too, and He, the Lord, is Intelligence Himself.

38. Two are the occasions when the Lord smiles. First, when brothers remove the chains which partition off the family property, saying, 'This is mine and that is thine;' and secondly, when the patient is on the point of death, and the physician says, 'I will cure him.'

39. Lunatics, drunkards, and children sometimes give out the truth unconsciously, as if inspired by Heaven.

40. The sun is many times larger than the earth, but owing to the great distance it appears like a small disk. So the Lord is infinitely great, but owing to our being too far from

Him we fall very, very short of comprehending His real greatness.

41. Knowingly or unknowingly, consciously or unconsciously, in whatever state we utter His name, we acquire the merit of such utterance. A man who voluntarily goes into a river and bathes therein gets the benefit of the bath; so does likewise he who has been pushed into the river by another, or who while sleeping soundly has water thrown upon him by another.

42. Satan never enters the house wherein are always sung the praises of Hari.

43. A king having committed the mortal crime of killing a Brāhmana, went to the hermitage of a sage to learn what penance he must perform in order to be purified. The sage was absent from home, but his son was there. The son hearing the case of the king, said, 'Repeat the name of God (Rama) three times and your sin will be expiated.' When the sage came back and heard the penance prescribed by his son, he said to him in great wrath, 'Sins committed in myriads of births are purged at once by but once uttering the name of the Almighty; how weak must be thy faith, O son, that thou hast ordered that name to be repeated thrice! For this offence of thine go and become a *Kandala*.' And the son became the Guhaka *Kandala* of the Ramayana.

44. Consciously or unconsciously, in whatever way one falls into the trough of nectar, one becomes immortal. Similarly, whosoever utters the name of the Deity voluntarily or involuntarily finds immortality in the end.

45. As a large and powerful steamer moves swiftly over the waters, towing rafts and barges in its wake, so when a Saviour descends, He easily carries thousands across the ocean of Māyā (illusion).

46. When the flood comes, it overflows rivers and streams, and makes one watery surface of all adjacent lands. But the rain-water flows away through fixed channels. When the Saviour becomes incarnate, all are saved through His grace. The Siddhas (perfect ones) only save themselves with much pain and penance.

47. When a mighty raft of wood floats down a stream, it can carry a hundred men, and still it does not sink. A reed floating down may sink with the weight of even a crow. So when a Saviour becomes incarnate, innumerable are the men who find salvation by taking refuge under Him. The Siddha only saves himself with much toil and trouble.

48. The locomotive engine reaches the destination itself, and also draws and takes with it a long train of loaded wagons. So likewise act the Saviours. They carry multitudes of men, heavily laden with the cares and sorrows of the world, to the feet of the Almighty.

49. When Bhagavan Sri Ramakandra came to this world, seven sages only could recognise Him to be the God incarnate. So when God descends into this world, few only can recognise His Divine nature.

50. On the tree of Sat-*k*it-ānanda there are innumerable Ramas, Krishnas, Christs, &c.; one or two of them come down into this world now and then, and produce mighty changes and revolutions.

51. The Avatara or Saviour is the messenger of God. He is like the Viceroy of a mighty monarch. As when there is some disturbance in a far-off province the king sends his viceroy to quell it; so whenever there is any waning of religion in any part of the world, God sends His Avatara there.

52. It is one and the same Avatara that, having plunged into the ocean of life, rises up in one place and is known as

Krishna, and diving again rises in another place and is known as Christ.

53. In some seasons water can be obtained from the great depths of the wells only and with great difficulty, but when the country is flooded in the rainy season, water is obtained with ease everywhere. So ordinarily, God is reached with great pains through prayers and penances, but when the flood of Incarnation descends, God is seen anywhere and everywhere.

54. A Siddha-purusha (perfect one) is like an archaeologist who removes the dust and lays open an old well which was covered up during ages of disuse by rank growth. The Avatara, on the other hand, is like a great engineer who sinks a new well in a place where there was no water before. Great men can give salvation to those only who have the waters of piety and goodness hidden in themselves, but the Saviour saves him too whose heart is devoid of all love, and dry as a desert.

55. Think not that Rāma, Sita, Śrī Krishna, *Rādhā*, Arguna, &c., were not historical personages, but mere allegories, or that the Scriptures have an inner and esoteric meaning only. Nay, they were human beings of flesh and blood just as you are, but because they were Divinities, their lives can be interpreted both historically and spiritually.

56. None knoweth the immensity of the sacrifice which the Godhead maketh when it becomes incarnate or becomes flesh.

57. The Saviours are to Brahman as the waves are to the ocean.

58. What is the state which a Siddha attains? (A perfect man and well-cooked food are both called siddha. There is a pun here on the word.) As potato or brinjal, &c., when boiled properly (Siddha), becomes soft and tender, so

when a man reaches perfection (Siddha) he becomes all humility and tenderness.

59. Five are the kinds of Siddhas found in this world:—

(1) The Svapna Siddhas are those who attain perfection by means of dream inspiration.

(2) The Mantra Siddhas are those who attain perfection by means of any sacred mantra.

(3) The Hathat Siddhas are those who attain perfection suddenly. As a poor man may suddenly become rich by finding a hidden treasure, or by marrying into a rich family, so many sinners become pure all of a sudden, and enter the Kingdom of Heaven.

(4) The Kripā Siddhas are those who attain perfection through the tangible grace of the Almighty, as a poor man is made wealthy by the kindness of a king.

(5) The Nitya Siddhas are those who are ever-perfect. As a gourd or a pumpkin-creeper brings forth fruit first and then its flower, so the ever-perfect is born a Siddha, and all his seeming exertions after perfection are merely for the sake of setting examples to humanity.

60. There is a fabled species of birds called 'Homa,' which live so high up in the heavens, and so dearly love those regions, that they never condescend to come down to the earth. Even their eggs, which, when laid in the sky, begin to fall down to the earth attracted by gravity, are said to get hatched in the middle of their downward course and give birth to the young ones. The fledgelings at once find out that they are falling down, and immediately change their course and begin to fly up towards their home, drawn thither by instinct. Men such as Suka Deva, Narada, Jesus, Samkarakarya and others, are like those birds, who even in their boyhood give up all attachments to the things of

this world and betake themselves to the highest regions of true Knowledge and Divine Light. These men are called Nitya Siddhas.

61. The Divine sages form, as it were, the inner circle of God's nearest relatives. They are like friends, companions, kinsmen of God. Ordinary beings form the outer circle or are the creatures of God.

62. When the shell of an ordinary cocoa-nut is pierced through, the nail enters the kernel of the nut too. But in the case of the dry nut, the kernel becomes separate from the shell, and so when the shell is pierced the kernel is not touched. Jesus was like the dry nut, i.e. His inner soul was separate from His physical shell, and consequently the sufferings of the body did not affect Him.

63. Once a holy man, while passing through a crowded street, accidentally trod upon the toe of a wicked person. The wicked man, furious with rage, beat the Sadhu mercilessly, till he fell to the ground in a faint. His disciples took great pains and adopted various measures to bring him back to consciousness, and when they saw that he had recovered a little, one of them asked, 'Sir, do you recognise who is attending upon you?' The Sādhu replied, 'He who beat me.' A true Sādhu finds no distinction between a friend and a foe.

64. The swan can separate the milk from water; it drinks only the milk, leaving the water untouched. Other birds cannot do so. Similarly, God is intimately mixed up with Maya; ordinary men cannot see Him separately from Maya. Only the Paramahamsa (the great soul—here is a pun on the word 'hamsa,' which means both soul and swan) throws off Māyā, and takes up God only.

65. The wind carries the smell of the sandal-wood as well as that of ordure, but does not mix with either. Similarly, a perfect man lives in the world, but does not mix with it.

66. A perfect man is like a lotus-leaf in the water or like a mud-fish in the marsh. Neither of these is polluted by the element in which it lives.

67. As water passes under a bridge but never stagnates, so money passes through the hands of 'The Free' who never hoard it.

68. As a rope that is burnt retains its shape intact, but has become all ashes, so that nothing can be bound with it; similarly, the man who is emancipated retains the form of his egoism, but not an idea of vanity (Ahamkāra).

69. As an aquatic bird, such as a pelican, dives into water, but the water does not wet its plumage, so the perfect man lives in the world, but the world does not touch him.

70. When the head of a goat is severed from its body, the trunk moves about for some time, still showing the signs of life. Similarly, though the Ahamkāra (vanity or egoism) is beheaded in the perfect man, yet sufficient of its vitality is left to make such a man carry on the functions of physical life; but that much is not sufficient to bind him again to the world.

71. Ornaments cannot be made of pure gold. Some alloy must be mixed with it. A man totally devoid of Māyā will not survive more than twenty-one days. So long as the man has body, he must have some Māyā, however small it may be, to carry on the functions of the body.

72. In the play of hide-and-seek, if the player once succeeds in touching the non-player, called the grand-dame (Boorī), he is no longer liable to be made a thief. Similarly, by once seeing the Almighty, a man is no longer bound down by the fetters of the world. The boy, by touching the Boorī, is free to go wherever he wishes, without being pursued, and no one can make him a thief. Similarly, in this world's playground, there is no fear to him who has once touched the feet of the Almighty.

73. The iron, once converted into gold by the touch of the Philosopher's stone, may be kept under the ground, or thrown into a rubbish-heap, but it remains always gold, and will never return to its former condition. Similar is the case with him who has once touched the feet of the Almighty. Whether he dwells in the bustle of the world, or in the solitude of forests, nothing will ever contaminate him.

74. The steel sword turns into a golden sword by the touch of the Philosopher's stone, and though it retains its former form it becomes incapable of injuring any one. Similarly, the outward form of a man who has touched the feet of the Almighty is not changed, but he no longer doeth any evil.

75. The loadstone rock under the sea attracts the ship sailing over it, draws out all its iron nails, separates its planks, and sinks the vessel into the deep. Thus, when the human soul is attracted by the magnetism of Universal Consciousness, the latter destroys in a moment all its individuality and selfishness, and plunges it in the ocean of God's infinite Love.

76. Milk and water, when brought into contact, are sure to mix so that the milk can never be separated again. So, if the neophyte, thirsting after self-improvement, mixes indiscriminately with all sorts of worldly men, he not only loses his ideals, but his former faith, love, and enthusiasm also die away imperceptibly. When, however, you convert the milk into butter, it no longer mixes with water, but floats over it. Similarly, when the soul once attains Godhead, it may live in any company, without ever being affected by its evil influences.

77. So long as no child is born to her, the newly-married girl remains deeply absorbed in her domestic duties. But no sooner is a son born, than she leaves off all her household

concerns, and no longer finds any pleasure in them. On the contrary, she fondles the newborn baby the livelong day, and kisses it with intense joy. Thus man, in his state of ignorance, performs all sorts of worldly works, but no sooner does he see the Almighty, than he finds no longer any relish in them. On the contrary, his happiness now consists only in serving the Deity and doing His works alone.

78. So long as a man is far from the market, he hears a loud and indistinct buzzing only, something like 'Ho! Ho!' But when he enters the market he no longer hears the uproar, but perceives distinctly that someone is bargaining for potatoes, another for Brinjal, and so on. As long as a man is far away from God, he is in the midst of the noise and confusion of reason, argument, and discussion; but when once a person approaches the Almighty, all reasonings, arguments, and discussions cease, and he understands the mysteries of God with vivid and clear perception.

79. So long as a man calls aloud, 'Allah Ho! Allah Ho! (O God! O God!), be sure that he has not found God, for he who has found him becomes still.

80. So long as the bee is outside the petals of the lotus, and has not tasted its honey, it hovers round the flower, emitting its buzzing sound; but when it is inside the flower, it drinks its nectar noiselessly. So long as a man quarrels and disputes about doctrines and dogmas, he has not tasted the nectar of true faith; when he has tasted it, he becomes still.

81. Little children play with dolls in a room apart just as they like, but as soon as their mother comes in they throw aside the dolls and run to her crying, 'Mamma, Mamma!' You also are now playing in this world deeply absorbed with the dolls of wealth, honour, and fame, and have no fear or anxiety. But if you once see the Divine Mother entering

in, you will not find pleasure any more in wealth, honour, and fame. Leaving off all these you will run to Her.

82. The naked Sage, Totapuri, used to say, 'If a brass pot be not rubbed daily, it will get rusty. So if a man does not contemplate the Deity daily, his heart will grow impure.' To him Sri Rāmakṛishna replied, 'Yes, but if the vessel be of gold, it does not require daily cleaning. The man who has reached God requires prayers or penances no more.'

83. He who has once tasted the refined and crystalline sugar-candy, finds no pleasure in raw treacle; he who has slept in a palace, will not find pleasure in lying down in a dirty hovel. So the soul that has once tasted the sweetness of the Divine Bliss finds no delight in the ignoble pleasures of the world.

84. She who has a king for her lover will not accept the homage of a street beggar. So the soul that has once found favour in the sight of the Lord does not want the paltry things of this world.

85. When a man is in the plains he sees the lowly grass and the mighty pine-tree and says, 'How big is the tree and how small is the grass!' But when he ascends the mountain and looks from its high peak to the plain below, the mighty pine-tree and the lowly grass blend into one indistinct mass of green verdure. So in the sight of worldly men there are differences of rank and position, but when the Divine sight is opened there remains no distinction of high and low.

86. When water is poured into an empty vessel a bubbling noise ensues, but when the vessel is full no such noise is heard. Similarly, the man who has not found God is full of vain disputations. But when he has seen Him, all vanities disappear, and he silently enjoys the Bliss Divine.

87. A woman naturally feels shy to relate to all the talk she daily has with her husband, save to her own companions.

Similarly, a devotee does not like to relate to anyone but a true Bhakta (devotee) the ecstatic joys which he experiences in his Divine communion; nay, sometimes he becomes impatient of relating his experiences even to those of his own class.

88. The moth once seeing the light never returns to darkness; the ant dies in the sugar-heap, but never retreats therefrom. Similarly, a good devotee gladly sacrifices his life for his God by renunciation.

89. Why does the God-lover find such pleasure in addressing the Deity as Mother? Because the child is more free with its mother, and consequently she is dearer to the child than anyone else.

90. The pious man, like a hemp-smoker, finds no pleasure in singing the praises of the Almighty alone. (The hemp-smoker never finds pleasure in smoking alone.)

91. If a strange animal enters a herd of cows, it is driven off by the combined attacks of the whole herd. But let only a cow enter, and all the other cows will make friends with her by mutual licking of bodies. Thus, when a devotee meets with another devotee, both experience great happiness and feel loth to separate, but when a scoffer enters the circle they carefully avoid him.

92. What is the strength of a devotee? He is a child of God, and tears are his greatest strength.

93. The young of a monkey clasps and clings to its mother. The young kitten cannot clasp its mother, but mews piteously whenever it is near her. If the young monkey lets go its hold on its mother, it falls down and gets hurt. This is because it depends upon its own strength; but the kitten runs no such risk, as the mother herself carries it about from place to place. Such is the difference between self-reliance and entire resignation to the will of God.

94. It is fabled that the pearl oyster leaves its bed at the bottom of the sea and comes up to the surface to catch the rain-water when the star Svati is in the ascendant. It floats about on the surface of the sea with its mouth agape, until it succeeds in catching a drop of the marvellous Svati-rain. Then it dives down to its sea-bed and there rests, till it has succeeded in fashioning a beautiful pearl out of that rain-drop. Similarly, there are some true and eager aspirants who travel from place to place in search of that watchword from a godly and perfect preceptor (Sad-guru) which will open for them the gate of eternal bliss, and if in their diligent search one is fortunate enough to meet such a Guru and get from him the much-longed-for *logos*, which is sure to break down all fetters, he at once retires from society, enters into the deep recess of his own heart and rests there, till he has succeeded in gaining eternal peace.

95. The flint may remain for myriads of years under water, still it does not lose its inner fire. Strike it with iron whenever you like and out flows the glowing spark. So is the true devotee firm in his faith. Though he may remain surrounded by all the impurities of the world, he never loses his faith and love. He becomes entranced as soon as he hears the name of the Almighty.

96. The Stone may remain for myriads of years in water, and the water will never penetrate it. But clay is soon softened into mud by the contact of water. So the strong heart of the faithful does not despair in the midst of trials and persecutions, but the man of weak faith is easily shaken even by the most trifling cause.

97. How sweet is the simplicity of the child! He prefers a doll to all riches and wealth. So is the faithful devotee. No one else can throw aside wealth and honour to take God only.

98. God is like unto a hill of sugar. A small ant carries away from it a small grain of sugar, the bigger ant takes from it a larger grain. But the hill remains as large as before. So are the devotees of God. They become ecstatic with even a grain of one Divine attribute. No one can contain within him all His attributes.

99. A logician once asked Sri Rāmakṛishna, 'What are knowledge, knower, and the object known?' To which he replied, 'Good man, I do not know all these niceties of scholastic learning. I know only my Mother Divine, and that I am Her son.'

100. A man who finds all the hairs of his body standing on end at the bare mention of Śrī Hari's name, through sheer ecstasy, and who sheds tears of love on hearing the name of God, he has reached his last birth.

101. The more you scratch the ringworm, the greater grows the itching, and the more pleasure do you find in scratching. Similarly, the devotees once beginning to sing His praises, never get tired of it, but continue for hours and hours together.

102. When grains are measured out to the purchaser in the granary of a rich merchant, the measurer unceasingly goes on measuring, while the attending women supply him with basket-fullṣ of grain from the main store. The measurer does not leave his seat, while the women incessantly supply him with grain. But a small grocer has neither such attendants, nor is his store so inexhaustible. Similarly, it is God Himself who is constantly inspiring thoughts and sentiments in the hearts of His devotees, and that is the reason why the latter are never in lack of new and wise thoughts and sentiments; while, on the other hand, the book-learned, like petty grocers, soon find that their thoughts have become exhausted.

103. A born farmer does not leave off tilling the soil, though it may not rain for twelve consecutive years, while a merchant who has but lately taken himself to the plough is discouraged by one season of drought. The true believer is never discouraged, if even with his lifelong devotion he fails to see God.

104. A true devotee who has drunk deep of the Divine Love is like a veritable drunkard, and, as such, cannot always observe the rules of propriety.

105. Dala (sedge) does not grow in large and pure water-tanks, but in small stagnant and miasmatic pools. Similarly, Dala (schism) does not take place in a party whose adherents are guided by pure, broad, and unselfish motives, but it takes firm root in a party whose advocates are given to selfishness, insincerity, and bigotry. ('Dala,' in Bengali, means both sedges and schism.)

106. The Yogins and Saṃnyāsins are like snakes. The snake never digs a hole for itself, but it lives in the hole made by the mouse. When one hole becomes uninhabitable, it enters into another hole. So the Yogins and the Saṃnyāsins make no houses for themselves; they pass their days in other men's houses—to-day in one house, to-morrow in another.

107. The sage alone can recognise a sage. He who deals in cotton twists can alone tell of what number and quality a particular twist is made.

108. A sage was lying in a deep trance (Samādhi) by a roadside; a thief passing by, saw him, and thought within himself, 'This fellow, lying here, is a thief. He has been breaking into some house by night, and now sleeps exhausted. The police will very soon be here to catch him. So let me escape in time.' Thus thinking, he ran away. Soon after a drunkard came upon the sage, and said, 'Hallo! thou hast fallen into the ditch by taking a drop too much. I am

steadier than thou, and am not going to tumble.' Last of all came a sage, and understanding that a great sage was in a trance (Samâdhi), he sat down, and touched him, and began to rub gently his holy feet.

109. An itinerant (Samādhi) came once upon the Kālī temple of Rāni Rāsamani, and seeing a dog eating the remains of a feast, he went up to him and said, embracing him, 'Brother, how is it that thou eatest alone, without giving me a share?' So saying, he began to eat along with the dog. The people of the place naturally thought him mad, but when standing before the temple of the Goddess, he began to chant forth some hymns in praise of Kālī, and the temple appeared to shake through the fervour of his devotion. Then the people knew him to be a great Sādhu. The true Sādhus roam about like children or mad men, in dirty clothes, and various other disguises.

110. The true religious man is he who does not do anything wrong or act impiously when he is alone, i.e. when there is none to look after and blame him.

111. In the Bengali alphabet no three letters are alike in sound except the three sibilants (Sa, sha, and sa), all meaning 'forbear,' 'forbear,' 'forbear.' This shows that even from our childhood we are made to learn forbearance in our very alphabets. The quality of forbearance is of the highest importance to every man.

112. Sugar and sand may be mixed together, but the ant rejects the sand and goes off with the sugar-grain; so pious men sift the good from the bad.

113. It is the nature of the winnowing basket to reject the bad and keep the good; even such is the case with pious men.

114. He is truly a pious man who is dead even in life, i.e. whose passions and desires have been all destroyed as in a dead body.

115. Worldly persons perform many pious and charitable acts with a hope of worldly rewards, but when misfortune, sorrow, and poverty approach them, they forget them all. They are like the parrot that repeats the Divine name 'Rādhā-Krishna, Rādhā-Krishna' the livelong day, but cries 'Kaw, Kaw' when caught by a cat, forgetting the Divine name.

116. A spring cushion is squeezed down when one sits upon it, but it soon resumes its original shape when the pressure is removed. So it is with worldly men. They are full of religious sentiments, so long as they hear religious talks; but no sooner do they enter into the daily routine of the world, than they forget all those high and noble thoughts, and become as impure as before.

117. So long as the iron is in the furnace it is red-hot, but it becomes black as soon as it is taken out of the fire. So also is the worldly man. As long as he is in church or in the society of pious people, he is full of religious emotions, but no sooner does he come out of those associations than he loses them all.

118. Someone said, 'When my boy Harish grows up, I will get him married, and give him the charge of the family; I shall then renounce the world, and begin to practise Yoga.' At this a Sādhu remarked, 'You will never find any opportunity of practising Yoga (devotion). You will say afterwards, "Harish and Girish are too much attached to me. They do not like to leave my company as yet." Then you will desire perhaps, "Let Harish have a son, and let me see that son married." And thus there will be no end of your desires.'

119. Flies sit at times on the sweetmeats kept exposed for sale in the shop of a confectioner; but no sooner does a sweeper pass by with a basket full of filth than the flies leave the sweetmeats and sit upon the filth-basket. But the

honey-bee never sits on filthy objects, and always drinks honey from the flowers. The worldly men are like flies. At times they get a momentary taste of Divine sweetness, but their natural tendency for filth soon brings them back to the dunghill of the world. The good man, on the other hand, is always absorbed in the beatific contemplation of Divine Beauty.

N.B. The worldly man is like a filthy worm that always lives and dies in filth, and has no idea of higher things; the good man of the world is like the fly that sits now on the filth and now on the sweet; while the free soul of a Yogin is like the bee that always drinks the honey of God's holy presence, and nothing else.

120. When it was argued that a family-man (G*ri*hastha) may remain in the family, but may have no concern with it, and consequently may remain uncontaminated by the world, an illustration was cited to refute such an argument, which is as follows:

A poor Brāhmana once came to one of those family-men, who are unconcerned with family affairs, to beg some money. When the beggar asked of him some money, he replied, 'Sir, I never touch money. Why are you wasting your time in begging of me?' The Brāhmana, however, would not go away. Tired with his importunate entreaties the man at last resolved in his mind to give him a rupee, and told him, 'Well, sir, come to-morrow, I shall see what I can do for you.' Then going in, this typical family-man told his wife, who was the manager of all his affairs, he being unconcerned, 'Look here, dear, a poor Brāhmana is in great difficulty, and wants something of me. I have made up my mind to give him a rupee. What is your opinion about it?' 'Aha! what a generous fellow you are!' she replied, in great excitement at the name of a rupee. 'Rupees are not, like leaves or stones, to be thrown away without any thought.' 'Well, dear,' replied the husband, in an apologising tone, 'the man is very poor and we should not give him less than a rupee.' 'No!' replied the wife, 'I cannot spare that much; here is a two-anna-bit and you can give him that, if you like.' The man of course had no other alternative, being himself unconcerned in all such worldly matters, and he took what his wife gave him. Next day the beggar came, and received only a two-anna-bit. Such uncontaminated family-men are really henpecked persons who are solely guided by their wives, and as such are very poor specimens of humanity.

121. Seeing the water pass glittering through the net of bamboo frame-work[1], the small fry enter into it with great pleasure, and having once entered they cannot get out again—and are caught. Similarly, foolish men enter into the world allured by its false glitter, but as it is easier to enter the net than to get out of it, it is easier to enter the world than renounce it, after having once entered it.

122. Men always quote the example of the king Ganaka, as that of a man who lived in the world and yet attained perfection. But throughout the whole history of mankind there is only this solitary example. His case was not the rule, but the exception. The general rule is that no one can attain spiritual perfection unless he renounces lust and greed. Do not think yourself to be a Ganaka. Many centuries have rolled away and the world has not produced another Ganaka.

123. This world is like a stage, where men perform many parts under various disguises. They do not like to take off the mask, unless they have played for some time. Let them play for a while, and then they will leave off the mask of their own accord.

---

1. A trap for catching small fish.

124. The heart of the devotee is like a dry match; and the slightest mention of the name of the Deity kindles the fire of love in his heart. But the mind of the worldly, soaked in lust and greed, is like the moist match, and can never be heated to enthusiasm, though God may be preached to him innumerable times.

125. A worldly man may be endowed with intellect as great as that of Ganaka, may take as much pains and trouble as a Yogin, and make as great sacrifices as an ascetic; but all these he makes and does, not for God, but for worldliness, honour, and wealth.

126. As water does not enter into a stone, so religious advice produces no impression on the heart of a worldly man.

127. As a nail cannot enter into a stone, but can easily be driven into the earth, so the advice of the pious does not affect the soul of a worldly man. It enters into the heart of a believer.

128. As soft clay easily takes an impression, but not so a stone, so also the Divine Wisdom impresses itself on the heart of the devotee, but not on the soul of the worldly man.

129. The characteristic of a thoroughly worldly man is that he does not only not listen to hymns, religious discourses, praises of the Almighty, &c., but also prevents others from hearing them, and abuses religious men and societies, and scoffs at prayers.

130. The alligator has got such a thick and scaly hide that no weapons can pierce it; on the contrary, they fall off harmless. So, howmuchsoever you may preach religion to a worldly man, it will have no effect upon his heart.

131. As the water enters in on one side under the bridge, and soon passes out on the other, so religious advice affects worldly souls. It enters into them by one ear and goes out

by the other, without making any impression upon their minds.

132. By talking with a worldly man one can feel that his heart is filled with worldly thoughts and desires, even as the crop of a pigeon is filled with grains.

133. So long as the fire is beneath, the milk boils and bubbles. Remove the fire and it is quiet again. So the heart of the neophyte boils with enthusiasm, so long as he goes on with his spiritual exercises, but afterwards it cools down.

134. As to approach a monarch one must ingratiate oneself with the officials that keep the gate and surround the throne, so to reach the Almighty one must practise many devotions, as well as serve many devotees and keep the company of the wise.

135. Keep thy own sentiments and faith to thyself. Do not talk about them abroad. Otherwise thou wilt be a great loser.

136. There are three kinds of dolls; the first made of salt, the second made of cloth, and the third made of stone. If these dolls be immersed in water, the first will get dissolved and lose its form, the second will absorb a large quantity of water but retain its form, while the third will be impervious to the water. The first doll represents the man who merges his self in the Universal and All-pervading Self and becomes one with it, that is the 'Mukta purusha'; the second represents a true lover or Bhakta, who is full of Divine bliss and knowledge; and the third represents a worldly man, who will not absorb the least drop of true knowledge.

137. As when fishes are caught in a net some do not struggle at all, some again struggle hard to come out of the net, while a few are happy enough to effect their escape by rending the net; so there are three sorts of men, viz. fettered (Baddha), wriggling (Mumukshu), and released (Mukta).

138. As sieves separate the finer and coarser parts of a pulverized or ground substance, keeping the coarser and rejecting the finer, even so the wicked man takes the evil and rejects the good.

139. Two men went into a garden. The worldly-wise man no sooner entered the gate than he began to count the number of the mango-trees, how many mangoes each tree bore, and what might be the approximate price of the whole orchard. The other went to the owner, made his acquaintance, and quietly going under a mango-tree began to pluck the fruit and eat it with the owner's consent. Now who is the wiser of the two? Eat mangoes, it will satisfy your hunger. What is the good of counting the leaves and making vain calculations? The vain man of intellect is uselessly busy in finding out the 'why and wherefore' of creation, while the humble man of wisdom makes acquaintance with the Creator and enjoys Supreme Bliss in this world.

140. The vulture soars high up in the air, but all the while he is looking down into the charnel-pits in search of putrid carcasses. So the book-read pandits speak glibly and volubly about Divine Knowledge, but it is all mere talk, for all the while their mind is thinking about how to get money, respect, honour, power, &c., the vain guerdon of their learning.

141. Once a dispute arose in the court of the Maharajah of Burdwan among the learned men there, as to who was the greater Deity, Siva or Vishnu. Some gave preference to Siva, others to Vishnu. When the dispute grew hot a wise pandit remarked, addressing the Raja, 'Sire, I have neither met *Śiva* nor seen Vishnu; how can I say who is the greater of the two?' At this the dispute stopped, for none of the disputants really had seen the Deities. Similarly none should compare one Deity with another. When a man has

really seen a Deity, he comes to know that all the Deities are manifestations of one and the same Brahman.

142. As the elephant has two sets of teeth, the external tusks and the inner grinders, so the God-men, like Śrī Krishna, &c., act and behave to all appearances like common men, while their heart and soul rest far beyond the pale of Karman.

143. The Sādhu who distributes medicines, and uses intoxicants, is not a proper Sādhu; avoid the company of such.

144. A Brāhmana was laying down a garden, and looked after it day and night. One day a cow straying into the garden browsed away a mango sapling which was one of the most carefully-watched trees of the Brāhmana. The Brāhmana seeing the cow destroy his favourite plant gave it such a sound beating that it died of the injuries received, The news soon spread like wildfire that the Brāhmana killed the sacred animal.

Now the Brāhmana was a so-called *Vedantist*, and when taxed with the sin denied it, saying,—'No, I have not killed the cow; it is my hand that has done it, and as Indra is the presiding Deity of the hand, so if any one has incurred the guilt of killing the cow, it is Indra and not I.'

Indra in his Heaven heard all this, assumed the shape of an old Brāhmana, came to the owner of the garden, and said, 'Sir, whose garden is this?'

Brāhmana— Mine.'

Indra— 'It is a beautiful garden. You have got a skilful gardener, for see how neatly and artistically he has planted the trees!'

Brāhmana— Well, sir, that is also my work. The trees are planted under my personal supervision and direction.'

Indra—' Indeed! O, you are very clever. But who has laid out this road? It is very ably planned and neatly executed.'

Brāhmana—' All this has been done by me.'

Then Indra with joined hands said, 'When all these things are yours, and you take credit for all the works done in this garden, it is hard lines for poor Indra to be held responsible for the killing of the cow.'

145. If thou art in right earnest to be good and perfect, God will send the true and proper Master (Sad-Guru) to thee. Earnestness is the only thing necessary.

146. As when going to a strange country, one must abide by the directions of him who knows the way, while taking the advice of many may lead to confusion, so in trying to reach God one should follow implicitly the advice of one single Guru who knows the way to God.

147. Whoever can call on the Almighty with sincerity and intense earnestness needs no Guru. But such a man is rare, hence the necessity of a Guru or Guide. The Guru should be only one, but Upagurus (assistant Gurus) may be many. He from whom any thing whatsoever is learned is an Upaguru. The great Avadhūta had twenty-four such Gurus.

148. Many roads lead to Calcutta. A certain man started from his home in a distant village towards the metropolis. He asked a man on the road, 'What road must I take to reach Calcutta soon?' The man said, 'Follow this road.' Proceeding some distance, he met another man and asked him, 'Is this the shortest road to Calcutta?' The man replied, 'O, no! You must retrace your footsteps and take the road to your left.' The man did so. Going in that new road for some distance he met a third man who pointed him out another road to Calcutta. Thus the traveller made no progress, but spent the day in changing one road for another. As he wanted to reach Calcutta he should have stuck to the road pointed out to him by the first man.

Similarly those who want to reach God must follow one and one only Guide.

149. The disciple should never criticise his own Guru. He must implicitly obey whatever his Guru says. Says a Bengâli couplet:

Though my Guru may visit tavern and still,
My Guru is holy Rai Nityananda still.

150. The Guru is a mediator. He brings man and God together.

151. Take the pearl and throw the oyster-shell away. Follow the mantra (advice) given thee by thy Guru and throw out of consideration the human frailties of thy teacher.

152. Listen not, if any one criticises and censures thy Guru. Leave his presence at once.

153. As the moon is the uncle of every child, so God is the Father and Guide of the whole Humanity. (The children in Bengal call the moon their 'maternal uncle.')

154. A disciple, having firm faith in the infinite power of his Guru, walked over a river even by pronouncing his name. The Guru, seeing this, thought within himself, 'Well, is there such a power even in my name? Then I must be very great and powerful, no doubt!' The next day he also tried to walk over the river pronouncing 'I, I, I,' but no sooner had he stepped into the waters than he sank and was drowned. Faith can achieve miracles, while vanity or egoism is the death of man.

155. Gurus can be had by hundreds, but good Chelas (disciples) are very rare.

156. It is easy to utter 'do, re, mi, fa, sol, la, si,' by mouth, but not so easy to sing or play them on any instrument. So it is easy to talk religion, but it is difficult to act religion.

157. Common men talk bagfuls of religion, but act not a grain of it, while the wise man speaks little, but his whole life is a religion acted out.

158. What you wish others to do, do yourself.

159. Verily, verily, I say unto you, that he who yearns for God, finds Him.

160. The petals of the lotus drop off in time, but they leave scars behind. So when true knowledge comes egoism goes off, but its traces remain. These, however, are not at all active for evil.

161. There are two Egos in man, one ripe and the other unripe. The ripe Ego thinks, 'Nothing is mine; whatever I see, or feel, or hear, nay, even this body is not mine, I am always free and eternal.' The unripe Ego, on the contrary, thinks, 'This is my house, my room, my child, my wife, my body, &c.'

162. The cup in which garlic juice is kept retains the nasty odour, though it may be rubbed and scoured hundreds of times. Egohood also is such an obstinate creature. It never leaves us completely.

163. The leaves of the cocoa-palm fall off, but leave still their marks behind on the trunk. Similarly, so long as one has this body, there will remain the mark of egoism, how high soever a man may advance in spirituality. But these traces of egoism do not bind such men to the world nor cause their re-birth.

164. The sun can give heat and light to the whole world, but it can do nothing when the clouds are in the sky and shut out its rays, Similarly, so long as egoism is in the soul, God cannot shine upon the heart.

165. Vanity is like a heap of rubbish or ashes on which the water, as soon as it falls, dries away. Prayers and contemplations produce no effect upon the heart puffed up with vanity.

166. Of all the birds of the air the crow is considered to be the wisest, and he thinks himself so too. He never falls into a snare. He flies off at the slightest approach of danger,

and steals the food with the greatest dexterity. But all this wisdom can supply him with no better living than filth and foul matter. This is the result of his having the wisdom of the pettifogger.

167. Once upon a time conceit entered the heart of the Divine Sage Nārada, and he thought there was no greater devotee than himself. Reading his heart, the Lord Śrī Vishnu said, 'Nārada, go to such and such a place, there is a great Bhakta of mine there, and cultivate his acquaintance.' Nārada went there and found an agriculturist, who rose early in the morning, pronounced the name of Hari only once, and taking his plough went out to till the ground all day long. At night he went to bed after pronouncing the name of Hari once more. Nārada said within himself, 'How can this rustic be called a lover of God? I see him busily engaged in worldly duties, and he has no signs of a pious man in him.' Nārada then went back to the Lord and said all he thought of his new acquaintance. The Lord said, 'Nārada, take this cup full of oil, go round this city and come back with it, but beware lest a drop of it fall to the ground.' Nārada did as he was told, and on his return he was asked, 'Well, Nārada, how often did you remember me in your walk?' 'Not once, my Lord,' replied Nārada, 'and how could I when I had to watch this cup brimming over with oil?' The Lord then said, 'This one cup of oil did so divert your attention that even you did forget me altogether, but look to that rustic who, carrying the heavy load of a family, still remembers me twice every day.'

168. There are three kinds of love, selfish, mutual, and unselfish. The selfish love is the lowest. It only looks towards its own happiness, no matter whether the beloved suffers weal or woe. In mutual love the lover not only wants the happiness of his or her beloved, but has an eye towards his or her own happiness also. The unselfish love is of the highest kind. The lover only minds the welfare of the beloved.

169. A true lover sees his God as his nearest and dearest relative, just as the shepherd women of Vrindāvana saw in Śrī Krishna, not the Lord of the Universe (Gagannātha), but their own beloved (Gopînātha).

170. 'I must attain perfection in this life, yea, in three days I must find God; nay, with a single utterance of His name I will draw Him to me.' With such a violent love the Lord is attracted soon. The lukewarm lovers take ages to go to Him, if at all.

171. A lover and a knower of God were once passing through a forest. On their way they saw a tiger at a distance. The Jñānin or knower of God said, 'There is no reason why we should flee; the Almighty God will certainly protect us.' At this the lover said, 'No, brother, come let us run away. Why should we trouble the Lord for what can be accomplished by our own exertions?'

172. The Knowledge of God may be likened to a man, while the Love of God is like a woman. Knowledge has entry only up to the outer rooms of God, but no one can enter into the inner mysteries of God save a lover, for a woman has access even into the harem of the Almighty.

173. Knowledge and love of God are ultimately one and the same. There is no difference between pure knowledge and pure love.

174. A group of fisherwomen on their way home from a distant market held on an afternoon, were overtaken by a heavy hailstorm at nightfall in the middle of their way, and so were compelled to take shelter in a florist's house near at hand. Through the kindness of the florist they were allowed to sleep that night in one of his rooms, where some baskets of sweet-smelling flowers had been kept for supplying his customers. The atmosphere of the room was too good for the fisherwomen, and they could not, owing to it, get even a wink of sleep, till one of them

suggested a remedy by saying, 'Let each of us keep her empty basket of fish close to her nose, and thus prevent this troublesome smell of flowers from attacking our nostrils and killing our sleep.' Every one gladly agreed to the proposal, and did accordingly; and soon all began to snore. Such, indeed, is the power and influence of bad habits over all those who are addicted to them.

175. A tame mongoose had its home high up on the wall of a house. One end of a rope was tied to its neck, while the other end was fastened to a weight. The mongoose with the appendage runs and plays in the parlour or in the yard of the house, but no sooner does it get frightened than it at once runs up and hides itself in its home on the wall. But it cannot stay there long, as the weight at the other end of the rope draws it down, and it is constrained to leave its home. Similarly, a man has his home high up at the feet of the Almighty. Whenever he is frightened by adversity and misfortune he goes up to his God, his true home; but in a short time he is constrained to come down into the world by its irresistible attractions.

176. As Heloncha (*Hingcha repens*) should not be counted among pot-herbs, or sugar-candy among common sweets, because even a sick man can use them without injuring his health; or as the pranava is not to be counted as a word, but as Divinity itself; so the desires of holiness, devotion, and love are not to be reckoned as desires at all.

177. When the fruit grows the petals drop off of themselves. So when the Divinity in thee increases, the weakness of humanity in thee will vanish.

178. The new-born calf falls and tumbles down scores of times before it learns to stand steady. So in the path of devotion, the slips are many before success is achieved.

179. Some get tipsy with even a small glass of wine. Others require two or three bottles to make them intoxicated. But

both get equal and full pleasure of intoxication. Similarly, some devotees get intoxicated with celestial bliss by coming in direct contact with the Lord of the Universe, while others become full of ecstasy even by a glimpse of the Divine Glory. But both are equally fortunate, since both are deluged with Divine bliss.

180. The snake is very venomous. It bites when any one approaches to catch it. But the person who has learnt the snake-charm can not only catch a snake, but carries about several of them like so many ornaments. Similarly, he who has acquired spiritual knowledge can never be polluted by lust and greed.

181. When a man realises one of the following states he becomes perfect:—(1) All this am I; (2) All this art thou; (3) Thou the Master, and I the servant.

182. Thou shouldst sacrifice thy body, mind, and riches, to find God.

183. Humanity must die before Divinity manifests itself. But this Divinity must, in turn, die before the higher manifestation of the Blissful Mother takes place. It is on the bosom of dead Divinity (Śiva) that the Blissful Mother dances Her dance celestial.

184. He finds God the quickest whose yearning and concentration are the greatest.

185. Samādhi is the state of bliss which is experienced by a live fish which, being kept out of water for some time, is again put into it.

186. There are hills and mountains, dales and valleys, under the sea, but they are not visible from the surface. So in the state of Samādhi, when one floats upon the ocean of Sat-*k*it-ānanda, all human consciousness lies latent in him.

187. If you fill an earthen vessel with water, and set it apart upon a shelf, the water in it will dry up in a few days; but

if you place the same pot into water it will remain filled as long as it is kept there. Even such is the case with your love to the Lord God. Fill and enrich your bosom with the love of God for a time, and then employ yourself in other affairs, forgetting Him all the while, and then you are sure to find within a short time that your heart has become poor and vacant and devoid of that precious love. But if you keep your heart immersed always in the depth of that holy love, your heart is sure to remain ever full to overflowing with the Divine fervour of sacred love.

188. He who at the time of contemplation is entirely unconscious of everything outside, has acquired the perfection of contemplation.

189. A jar kept in water is full of water inside and outside. Similarly the soul immersed in God sees the all-pervading spirit within and without.

190. When the grace of the Almighty descends, everyone will understand his mistakes; knowing this you should not dispute.

191 The darkness of centuries is dispersed at once as soon as a light is brought into the room. The accumulated ignorances and misdoings of innumerable births vanish before the single glance of the Almighty's gracious look.

192. When the Malaya breeze blows, all trees, having stamina in them, become converted into sandal-trees; but those which have no stamina remain unchanged as before, like bamboo, plantain, palm-tree, &c. So when Divine Grace descends, men having the germs of piety and goodness in them are changed at once into holy beings and are filled with Divinity, but worthless and worldly men remain as before.

193. As the dawn heralds in the rising sun, so unselfishness, purity, righteousness, &c., precede the advent of the Lord.

194. As a king, before going to the house of his servant, sends from his own stores the necessary seats, ornaments, food, &c., to his servant, so that the latter may properly receive him; so before the Lord cometh, He sends love, reverence, faith, yearning, &c., into the heart of the devotee.

195. Shallow water in an open field will in time be dried up though no one may lessen it by using it. So a sinner is sometimes purified by simply resigning himself totally and absolutely to the mercy and grace of God.

196. A policeman can see with a dark lantern (bull's-eye) every one upon whom he throws the rays, but no one can see him so long as he does not turn the light towards himself. So does God see every one, but no one seeth Him until the Lord revealeth Himself to him in His mercy.

197. There are some fish which have many sets of bones, and others have one; but as the eater cleans all the bones and eats the fish, so some men have many sins and others have few; but the grace of God purifies them all in time.

198. The breeze of His grace is blowing night and day over thy head. Unfurl the sails of thy boat (mind) if thou wantest to make rapid progress through the ocean of life.

199. Fans should be discarded when the wind blows. Prayers and penances should be discarded when the grace of God descends.

200. Creeds and sects matter nothing. Let every one perform with faith the devotions and practices of his creed. Faith is the only clue to get to God.

201. He who has faith has all, and he who wants faith wants all.

202. The faith-healers of India order their patients to repeat with full conviction the words, 'There is no illness in me, there is no illness at all.' The patient repeats it, and, thus mentally denying, the illness goes off. So if you think yourself to be morally weak and without goodness, you

will really find yourself to be so in no time. Know and believe that you are of immense power, and the power will come to you at last.

203. Bhagavān Śrī Rāmachandra had to bridge the ocean before he could cross over to Lamkā (Ceylon). But Hanumān, his faithful monkey-servant, with one jump çrossed the ocean through the firmness of his faith in Rāma. Here the servant achieved more than the master, simply through faith.

204. A man wanted to cross the river. A sage gave him an amulet and said, This will carry thee across.' The man, taking it in his hand, began to walk over the waters. When he reached the middle of the river curiosity entered into his heart, and he opened the amulet to see what was in it. Therein he found, written on a bit of paper, the sacred name of Rāma. The man at this said deprecatingly, Is this the only secret?' No sooner had he said this than he sank down. It is faith in the name of the Lord that works miracles, for faith is life, and doubt is death.

205. *Q.* How can I perform devotion when I must always think of my daily bread? *A.* He for whom thou workest will supply thy necessities. God hath made provision for thy support before he sent thee here.

206. *Q.* When shall I be free? *A.* When thy I-hood (egoism) will vanish, and thy self-will be merged in the Divinity.

207. Out of the myriads of paper kites that are made to fly in the air, only one or two rend the string and get free. So out of hundreds of Sādhakas, only one or two get free from worldly bonds.

208. As a piece of lead, thrown into a basin of mercury, is soon dissolved therein, so the human soul loses its individual existence when it falls into the ocean of Brâhma.

209. *Q.* What do you say about the method of religious preaching employed now-a-days? *A.* It is inviting

hundreds of persons to dinner, when the food supply is sufficient for one only.

210. Instead of preaching to others, if one worships God all that time, that is enough preaching. He who strives to make himself free, is the real preacher. Hundreds come from all sides, no one knows whence, to him who is free, and are taught. When a flower opens the bees come from all sides uninvited and unasked.

211. Hast thou got, O preacher, the badge of authority? As the humblest subject wearing the badge of the King is heard with respect and awe, and can quell the riot by showing his badge; so must thou, O preacher, obtain first the order and inspiration from God. So long as thou hast not this inspiration, thou mayest preach all thy life, but that will be mere waste of breath.

212. He alone is the true 'man' who is illumined with the Spiritual Light.

213. The soul enchained is 'man,' and free from chain is 'Śiva' (God).

214. The heavier scale of a balance goes down while the lighter one rises up. Similarly he who is weighed down with too many cares and anxieties of the world, goes down to the world, while he who has less cares rises up towards the Kingdom of Heaven.

215. God is in all men, but all men are not in God: that is the reason why they suffer.

216. There are two sorts of men. The Guru said to one of his disciples, 'What I impart to thee, my dear, is invaluable; keep it to thyself,' and the disciple kept it all to himself. But when the Guru imparted that knowledge to another of his disciples, the latter, knowing its inestimable worth, and not liking to enjoy it all alone, stood upon a high place and began to declare the good tidings to all the people.

The Avatâras are of the latter class, while the Siddhas are of the former.

217. No man keeps a total fast. Some get food at 9 a.m., others at noon, others at 2 p.m., and others in the evening Similarly, at some time or other, in this life or after many lives, all will see God.

218. When fruit becomes ripe and falls of itself, it tastes very sweet; but when unripe fruit is plucked and artificially ripened it does not taste so sweet and becomes shrivelled up. So when one has attained perfection, the observance of caste distinctions falls off of itself from him, but so long as this exalted knowledge is not reached, one must observe caste distinctions.

219. When a storm blows, it is impossible to distinguish an Asvattha (pippal) and a Vata (banian) tree. So when the storm of true knowledge (the knowledge of one universal existence) blows, there can be no distinction of caste.

220. When a wound is perfectly healed, the slough falls off of itself; but if the slough be taken off earlier, it bleeds. Similarly, when the perfection of knowledge is reached by a man, the distinctions of caste fall off from him, but it is wrong for the ignorant to break such distinctions.

221. *Q*. Is it proper to keep the Brāhmanical thread? *A*. When the knowledge of self is obtained, all fetters fall off of themselves. Then there is no distinction of a Brāhmana Or a Sûdra, a high caste or a low caste. In that case the sacred thread-sign of caste falls away of itself. But so long as a man has the consciousness of distinction and difference he should not forcibly throw it off.

222. *Q*. Why do you not lead a family life with your wife? *A*. The God Kārtikeya, the leader of the Heavenly army, once happened to scratch a cat with his nail. On going home he saw there was the mark of a scratch on the cheek of his Mother. Seeing this, he asked of her, 'Mother, dear, how

have you got that ugly scratch on your cheek?' The Goddess Durgā replied, 'Child, this is thy own handiwork,—the mark scratched by thy own nail.' Kārtikeya asked in wonder, 'Mother, how is it? I never remember to have scratched thee!' The Mother replied, 'Darling, hast thou forgotten having scratched a cat this morning?' Kārtikeya said, 'Yes, I did scratch a cat; but how did your cheek get marked?' The Mother replied, 'Dear child, nothing exists in this world but myself. I am all creation. Whomsoever thou hurtest, thou hurtest me.' Kārtikeya was greatly surprised at this, and determined thenceforward never to marry; for whom would he marry? Every woman was mother to him. I am like Kārtikeya. I consider every woman as my Divine Mother.

223. When I look upon chaste women of respectable families, I see in them the Mother Divine arrayed in the garb of a chaste lady; and again, when I look upon the public women of the city, sitting in their open verandas, arrayed in the garb of immorality and shamelessness, I see in them also the Mother Divine, sporting in a different way.

224. The light of the gas illumines various localities with various intensities. But the life of the light, namely, the gas, comes from one common reservoir. So the religious teachers of all climes and ages are but as many lamp-posts through which is emitted the light of the spirit flowing constantly from one source, the Lord Almighty.

225. As the rain-water from the top of a house may be discharged through pipes having their mouth-pieces shaped like the head of a tiger, a cow or a bull, &c., although the water does not belong to these pipes, but comes from the heaven above, so are the holy Sādhus (saints) through whose mouths eternal and heavenly truths are discharged into this world by the Almighty.

226. The cries of all jackals are alike. The teachings of all the wise men of the world are essentially one and the same.

227. Whatever gives happiness in this world contains a bit of divine enjoyment in it. The difference between the two is as between treacle and refined candy.

228. He who is absorbed in others' affairs, forgets his own outer and inner affairs (i.e. does not think about his own lower and higher self, but is absorbed in the affairs of other selfs).

229. When the mind dwells in evil propensities, it is like a high-caste Brāhmana living in the quarters of the out-castes, or like a gentleman dwelling in the back slums of the town.

230. If a man sees a pleader he naturally thinks of cases and causes; similarly, on seeing a pious devotee, the man remembers his God and the hereafter.

231. *Q.* What is the reason that a Prophet is not honoured by his own kinsmen? *A.* The kinsmen of a juggler do not crowd round him to see his performances, while strangers stand agape at his wonderful tricks.

232. The seeds of Vagravāntula do not fall to the bottom of the tree. From the shell they shoot far away from the tree and take root there. So the Spirit of a Prophet manifests itself at a distance, and he is appreciated there.

233. There is always a shade under the lamp while its light illumines the surrounding objects. So the man in the immediate proximity of a Prophet does not understand him. Those who live afar off are charmed by his spirit and extraordinary power.

234. The waters of a swiftly-flowing current move round and round in eddies and whirlpools, but quickly crossing these they resume their former course. So the hearts of the pious fall sometimes into the whirlpools of despondency,

grief, and unbelief, but it is only a momentary aberration. It does not last long.

235. A tree, laden with fruit, always bends low. So, if thou wantest to be great, be low and meek.

236. The heavier scale goes down and the lighter one rises up. So the man of merit and ability is always humble, but the fool is always puffed up with vanity.

237. The anger of the good is like a line drawn on the surface of water, which does not last long.

238. If a white cloth is stained with a small speck the blackness appears very ugly indeed by the contrast; so the smallest fault of a holy man becomes painfully prominent by his surrounding purity.

239. The sunlight is one and the same wherever it falls; but bright surfaces like water, mirror and polished metals, &c., can reflect it fully. So is the Light Divine. It falls equally and impartially on all hearts, but the pure and clean hearts of the good and holy Sādhus only can fully reflect it.

240. As in a pane of glass on which quicksilver has been laid, one can see his face reflected, so in the chaste heart of a totally abstinent man is reflected the image of the Almighty.

241. So long as one does not become simple like a child, one does not get Divine illumination. Forget all the worldly knowledge that thou hast acquired, and become as ignorant about it as a child, and then thou wilt get the knowledge of the True.

242. The Hindu almanacs contain predictions of the annual rainfall. But squeeze the book, and not a drop of water will be got out of it. So also many good sayings are to be found in books, but merely reading them will not make one religious. One has to practise the virtues taught therein.

243. Q. Why do religions degenerate? A. The rain-water is pure, but becomes soiled according to the medium it passes through. If the roof and the pipe be dirty, the discharge is dirty.

244. Money can procure bread and butter only. Do not consider it therefore as if it were thy sole end and aim.

245. As by rubbing gold and brass on a touch-stone, their real worth becomes known; so a sincere Sādhu and a hypocrite are found out when they are rubbed through the touch-stone of persecution and adversity.

246. The iron must be heated several times and hammered before it becomes good steel. Then only it becomes fit to be made into a sharp sword, and can be bent any way you like. So a man must be heated several times in the furnace of tribulations, and hammered with the persecutions of the world, before he becomes pure and humble.

247. Remain always strong and steadfast in thy own faith, but eschew all bigotry and intolerance.

248. Be not like the frog in the well. The frog in the well knows nothing bigger and grander than its well. So are all bigots: they do not see anything better than their own creeds.

249. There was a man who worshipped Śiva, but hated all other Deities. One day Śiva appeared to him and said, 'I shall never be pleased with thee, so long as thou hatest the other gods.' But the man was inexorable. After a few days Śiva again appeared to him. This time he appeared as Hari-Hara, that is, one side of his body was that of Siva, and the other side that of Vishnu. At this the man was half pleased and half displeased. He laid his offerings on the side representing Śiva, and did not offer anything to the side representing Vishnu, and when he offered the burning incense to his beloved God (Śiva) he was careful as well as audacious enough to press the nostril of Vishnu, the other half of Hari-Hara, lest the fragrance

should be pleasing to Vishnu. Seeing him altogether inexorable, the God Siva was sorely displeased with him, and at once vanished from his sight. But the man was as undaunted as ever. However, the children of the village began to tease him by uttering the name of Vishnu in his hearing. Displeased with this, the man hung two bells to his ears, which he used to ring as soon as the boys cried out the names of Vishnu, in order to prevent the sound entering his ears. And thus he was known by the name of Bell-eared, or Ghantā-karna. He is still so much hated for his bigotry that every year at a certain period the boys of Bengal break down his effigy with a cudgel, and this serves him right.

250. As the young wife in a family shows her love and respect to her father-in-law, mother-in-law, and every other member of the family, and at the same time loves her husband more than these; similarly, being firm in thy devotion to the Deity of thy own choice (Ishta-Devatā), do not despise other Deities, but honour them all.

251. A truly religious man should think that other religions also are paths leading to the truth. We should always maintain an attitude of respect towards other religions.

252. The difference between the modern Brahmaism and Hinduism is like the difference between the single note of music and the whole music. The modern Brahmas are content with the single note of Brahman, while the Hindu religion is made up of several notes producing a sweet and melodious harmony.

253. Some years ago, when the Hindus and the Brāhmas were preaching their respective religions with true earnestness and great zeal, some one asked Bhagavān Śrī Rāmakrishna his opinion about both parties, on which he replied, I see that my Mother Divine is getting her work done through both parties.'

254. Hari (from hri, to steal) means 'He who steals our hearts,' and Haribala means 'Hari is our strength.'

255. Sin like quicksilver can never be kept concealed. (When a man takes calomel, sooner or later it is sure to show itself in the shape of eruptions on the skin.)

256. The tears of repentance and the tears of happiness flow from the two different corners of the eye. The tears of repentance flow from the side near the nose, and the tears of happiness flow from the other extremity.

257. Visit not miracle workers. They are wanderers from the path of truth. Their minds have become entangled in the meshes of psychic powers, which lie in the way of the pilgrim towards Brahman, as temptations. Beware of these powers, and desire them not.

258. A man after fourteen years of hard asceticism in a lonely forest obtained at last the power of walking over the waters. Overjoyed at this acquisition, he went to his Guru, and told him of his grand feat. At this the Master replied, 'My poor boy, what thou hast accomplished after fourteen years' arduous labour, ordinary men do the same by paying a penny to the boatman.'

259. A youthful disciple of Śrī Rāmakrishna once acquired the power of reading the heart of another. When he related this experience to the Master, he rebuked him and said, 'Shame on thee, child, do not waste thy energies on these petty things.'

260. A washerman keeps a large store of clothes and has a rich wardrobe, but these are not his. As soon as the clothes are washed his wardrobe becomes empty. Men having no original thoughts of their own are like the washerman.

261. Greed brings woe, while contentment is all happiness. A barber was once passing under a haunted tree when he heard a voice say, 'Wilt thou accept of seven jars of

gold?' The barber looked round, but could see no one. The mysterious voice again repeated the words, and the cupidity of the barber being greatly roused by the spontaneous offer of such vast wealth he spoke aloud, 'When the merciful God is so good as to take pity even on a poor barber like me, is there anything to be said as to my accepting the kind offer so generously made?' At once the reply came, 'Go home, I have already carried the jars thither.' The barber ran in hot haste to his house, and was transported to see the promised jars there. He opened them one after another and saw them all filled, save one which was half filled. Now arose the desire of filling this last jar in the heart of the barber. So he sold all his gold and silver ornaments and converted them into coins and threw them into the jar. But the jar still remained empty. He now began to starve himself and his family by living upon insufficient, coarse, and cheap food, throwing all his savings into the jar, but the jar remained as empty as ever. The barber then requested the King to increase his pay as it was not sufficient to maintain him and his family. As he was a favourite of the King, the latter granted his request. The barber now began to save all his pay and emoluments, and throw them all into the jar, but the greedy jar showed no sign of being filled. He now began to live by begging, and became as wretched and miserable as ever. One day the King seeing his sad plight, inquired of him by saying, 'Hallo! when thy pay was half of what thou gettest now, thou wast far happier and more cheerful, contented, and healthy, but with double that pay I see thee morose, care-worn, and dejected. Now what is the matter with thee? Hast thou accepted the seven jars of gold?' The barber was taken aback by this home-thrust, and with clasped hands asked the King as to who had informed his majesty about the matter. The King answered, 'Whosoever accepts the riches of a Yaksha is sure to be reduced to such an abject and wretched plight. I have known thee through this invariable sign. Do away with the money at once. Thou canst not spend a farthing of it. That money is for hoarding and not for spending.' The barber was brought to his senses by this advice and went to the haunted tree and said, 'O Yaksha, take back thy gold,' and he returned home to find the seven jars vanished, taking with them his life-long savings. Nevertheless he began to live happily after it.

262. It is very pleasant to scratch a ringworm, but the after-sensation is very painful and intolerable; so the pleasures of the world are very pleasant in the beginning, but their after-consequences are very terrible to contemplate.

263. *Q*. What is the world like? *A*. It is like an Amla fruit, all skin and stone with but very little pulp, the eating of which produces colic.

264. Like unto a miser that longeth after gold, let thy heart pant after Him.

265. So long as the heavenly expanse of the heart is troubled and disturbed by the gusts of desire, there is little chance of our beholding therein the brightness of God. The beatific vision occurs only in the heart which is calm and rapt up in divine communion.

266. The soiled mirror never reflects the rays of the sun, and the impure and unclean in heart who are subject to Māyā (illusion) never perceive the glory of the Bhagavān (the Venerable). But the pure in heart see the Lord, as the clear mirror reflects the sun. Be holy, then.

267. As on the troubled surface of rolling waters the moon shines in broken images, so on the unsettled mind of a worldly man engrossed in Māyā, the perfect God shines with partial light only.

268. Why does a Bhakta (one full of the love of God) forsake everything for the sake of God? An insect flies from the darkness as soon as any light meets its eyes; the ant loses its life in molasses, but never leaves them. So the Bhakta cleaves unto his God for ever, and leaves all else.

269. As one can ascend to the top of a house by means of a ladder or a bamboo or a staircase or a rope, so diverse also are the ways and means to approach God, and every religion in the world shows one of these ways.

270. If God is Omnipresent, why do we not see Him? Standing by the bank of a pool thickly overspread with scum and weeds, you will say that there is no water in it. If you desire to see the water, remove the scum from the surface of the pond. With eyes covered with the film of Māyā you complain that you cannot see God. If you wish to see Him, remove the film of Māyā from off your eyes.

271. Why cannot we see the Divine Mother? She is like a high-born lady transacting all her business from behind the screen, seeing all, but seen by none. Her devout sons only see Her, by going near Her and behind the screen of Māyā.

272. Dispute not. As you rest firmly on your own faith, allow others also the same liberty to stand by their own faiths. By mere disputation you shall never succeed in convincing another of his error. When the grace of God descends on him, every one will understand his own mistakes.

273. A husbandman was watering a sugar-cane field the whole of a day. After finishing his task he saw that not a drop of water had entered the field; all the water had gone underground through several big rat-holes. Such is the state of that devotee who, cherishing secretly in his heart worldly desires (of fame, pleasures, and comforts) and ambitions, worships God. Though daily praying, he makes no progress because the entire devotion runs to

waste through the rat-holes of his desires, and at the end of his life-long devotion he is the same man as before, and has not advanced one step.

274. Keep thyself aloof at the time of thy devotion from those who scoff, and those who ridicule piety and the pious.

275. Is it good to create sects? (Here is a pun on the word 'Dal,' which means both a 'sect' or 'party' as well as 'the rank growth on the surface of a stagnant pool.') The 'Dal' cannot grow in a current of water: it grows only in the stagnant waters of petty pools. He whose heart earnestly longs after the Deity has no time for anything else. He who looks for fame and honour, forms sects (Dal). (Cf. 105.)

276. The Vedas, Tantras, and the Puranas, and all the sacred scriptures of the world, have become as if defiled (as food thrown out of the mouth becomes polluted): because they have been constantly repeated by and have come out of human mouths. But the Brahman or the Absolute has never been defiled, for no one as yet has been able to express Him by human speech.

277. The parable of a Brahman and his low-caste servant:

As soon as Māyā is found out, she flies away. A priest was once going to the village of a disciple. He had no servant with him. On the way, seeing a cobbler, he addressed him, saying, 'Hallo! good man, wilt thou accompany me as a servant? Thou shalt dine well and wilt be cared for; come along.' The cobbler replied, Reverend Sir, I am of the lowest caste, how can I represent your servant?' The priest said, 'Never mind that. Do not tell anybody what thou art, nor speak to or make acquaintance with any one.' The cobbler agreed. At twilight, while the priest was sitting at prayers in the house of his disciple, another Brahman came and addressed the priest's servant, 'Fellow, go and bring my shoes from there.' The servant, true to the words of his master, made no response. The Brahman repeated the order a second time, but the servant remained silent. The Brahman repeated it again and again, but the cobbler moved not an inch. At last, getting annoyed, the Brahman angrily said, 'Hallo Sirrah! How darest thou not obey a Brahman's command! What is thy caste? Art thou not a cobbler?' The cobbler hearing this began to tremble with fear, and piteously looking at the priest said, '0 venerable Sir, O venerable Sir! I am found out. I cannot stay here any longer, let me flee.' So saying he took to his heels.

278. What is the relation between Gīvātman and Paramātman, the personal and the Highest Self?

As when a plank of wood is stretched across a current of water, the water seems to be divided into two, so the indivisible appears divided into two by limitations (Upādhi) of Māyā. In truth they are one and the same.

279. There is little chance of a ship running astray, so long as its compass points towards the true North. So if the mind of man—the compass-needle of the ship of life is turned always towards the Parabrahman without oscillation, it will steer clear of every danger.

280. The Avadhūta saw a bridal procession passing through a meadow, with the beating of drums and the blowing of trumpets, and with great pomp. Hard by the road through which the procession was passing he saw a hunter deeply absorbed in aiming at a bird, and perfectly inattentive to the noise and pomp of the procession, casting not even a passing look at it. The Avadhūta, saluting the hunter, said, 'Sir, you are my Guru. When I sit in meditation let my mind be concentrated on its object of meditation as yours has been on the bird.'

281. An angler was fishing in a pond. The Avadhūta, approaching him, asked, 'Brother, which way leads to such and such a place?' The float of the rod at that time was

indicating that the fish was nibbling the bait: so the man did not give any reply, but was all attention to his fishing-rod. When the fish was caught, he turned round and said, 'What is it you have been saying, sir?' The Avadhūta saluted him and said, 'Sir, you are my Guru. When I sit in the contemplation of the Paramātman, let me follow your example, and before finishing my devotions let me not attend to anything else.'

282. A heron was slowly walking to catch a fish. Behind, there was a hunter aiming an arrow at it; but the bird was totally unmindful of this fact. The Avadhūta, saluting the heron, said, 'When I sit in meditation let me follow your example, and never turn back to see who is behind me.'

283. A kite with a fish in its beak was followed by a host of crows and other kites, which were screeching and pecking at it, and were trying to snatch the fish away. In whatever direction it went the crowd of kites and crows followed it, screeching and cawing. Getting tired of this annoyance, the kite let go the fish, when it was instantly caught by another kite, and at once the crowd of kites and crows transferred their kind attentions to the new owner of the fish. The first kite was left unmolested, and sat calmly on the branch of a tree. Seeing this quiet and tranquil state of the bird the Avadhūta, saluting it, said, 'You are my Guru, O Kite; for you have taught me that so long as man does not throw off the burden of the worldly desires he carries, he cannot be undisturbed and at peace with himself.'

284. The human Guru whispers the sacred formula into the ear; the Divine Guru breathes the spirit into the soul.

285. If thou wishest to thread the needle, make the thread pointed, and remove all extraneous fibres. Then the thread will easily enter into the eye of the needle. So if thou wishest to concentrate thy heart on God, be meek,

humble, and poor in spirit, and remove all filaments of desire.

286. A snake dwelt in a certain place. No one dared to pass by that way. For whoever did so was instantaneously bitten to death. Once a Mahātman passed by that road, and the serpent ran after the sage in order to bite him. But when the snake approached the holy man he lost all his ferocity, and was overpowered by the gentleness of the Yogin. Seeing the snake, the sage said, 'Well, friend, thinkest thou to bite me?' The snake was abashed and made no reply. At this the sage said, 'Hearken, friend, do not injure anybody in future.' The snake bowed and nodded assent. The sage went his own way and the snake entered his hole, and thenceforward began to live a life of innocence and purity without even attempting to harm any one. In a few days all the neighbourhood began to think that the snake had lost all his venom, and was no more dangerous, and so every one began to tease him. Some pelted him, others dragged him mercilessly by the tail, and in this way there was no end to his troubles. Fortunately the sage again passed by that way, and seeing the bruised and battered condition of the good snake, was very much moved, and inquired the cause of his distress. At this the snake replied, 'Holy sir, this is because I do not injure any one, after your advice. But alas! they are so merciless!' The sage smilingly said, 'My dear friend, I simply advised you not to bite any one, but I did not tell you not to frighten others. Although you should not bite any creature, still you should keep every one at a considerable distance by hissing at him.'

Similarly, if thou livest in the world, make thyself feared and respected. Do not injure any one, but be not, at the same time, injured by others.

287. When the bird has flown away from it, one cares no longer for the cage. So when the bird of life has flown away, no one cares any longer for the carcase.

288. As a lamp does not burn without oil, so a man cannot live without God.

289, 290. A learned Brahman once went over to a wise king and said, 'Hear, O king, I am well versed in the holy scriptures. I intend to teach thee the holy book of the Bhāgavata.' The king, who was the wiser of the two, well knew that a man who has read the Bhāgavata would seek more to know his own Self than honour and wealth in a king's court. He replied, 'I see, O Brahman, that you yourself have not mastered that book thoroughly. I promise to make you my tutor, but go first and learn the scripture well.' The Brahman went his way, thinking within himself, 'How foolish the king is to say I have not mastered the Bhāgavata well, when I have been reading the book over and over again for all these years.' However, he went over the book carefully once more and appeared before the king. The king told him the same thing again and sent him away. The Brahman was sore vexed, but thought there must be some meaning for this behaviour of the king. He went home, shut himself up in his closet, and applied himself more than ever to the study of the book. By and by the hidden meanings began to flash before his intellect; the vanity of running after the bubbles, riches and honour, kings and courts, wealth and fame, all vanished before his unclouded vision. From that day forward he gave himself up entirely to attain perfection by the worship of God, and never returned to the king. A few years after the king thought of the Brahman, and went to his house to see what he was about. Seeing the Brahman, all radiant with the divine light and love, he fell upon his knees and said, 'I see you have now arrived at the true meaning of the scriptures; I am ready to be your disciple, if you will duly condescend to make me one.'

291. As long as there is no breeze blowing, we fan ourselves to alleviate heat, but when the breeze blows both for rich and poor, we give up fanning. We should persevere ourselves to reach our final goal as long as there is no help from above; but when that help comes to any, let him then stop labouring and persevering; otherwise not.

292. *Q*. Where is God? How can we get to Him? *A*. There are pearls in the sea, you must dive deep again and again until you get the pearls. So there is God in the world, but you should persevere to see Him.

293. How does the soul stay in the body? As the piston stays in a syringe.

294. As in mid-ocean a bird, which found its perch upon the topmast of a ship, getting tired of its position, flies away to discover a new place of rest for itself, and alas! without finding any, returns at last to its old roost upon the masthead, weary and exhausted; so when an ordinary aspirant, being disgusted with the monotony of the task and the discipline imposed upon him by his well-wishing and thoroughly experienced preceptor (Guru), loses all hope, and, having no confidence in him, launches forth into the broad world ever in search of a new adviser, he is sure at last to return to his original master after a fruitless search, which has, however, increased the reverence of the repentant aspirant for the master.

295. In the month of June a young goat was playing near his mother, when, with a merry frisk, he told her that he meant to make a feast of Ras-flowers, a species of flowers budding abundantly during the time of the Rāslīlā festival. 'Well, my darling,' replied the dam, 'it is not such an easy thing as you seem to think. You will have to pass through many crises before you can hope to feast on Ras-

flowers. The interval between the coming September and October is not very auspicious to you; for some one may take you for a sacrifice to the Goddess Durgā; then, again, you will have to get through the time of Kālī-pūjā, and if you are fortunate enough to escape through that period, there comes the Gagaddhātri-pūjā, when almost all the surviving male members of our tribe are destroyed. If your good luck leads you safe and sound through all these crises, then you can hope to make a feast of Ras-flowers in the beginning of November.' Like the dam in the fable, we should not hastily approve of all the aspirations which our youthful hopes may entertain, remembering the manifold crises which one will have to pass through in the course of one's life.

296. As the fly sits, now on the unclean sore of the human body, and now on the offerings dedicated to the gods, so the mind of the worldly man is at one time deeply engaged in religious topics and at the next moment loses itself in the pleasures of wealth and lust.

297. As the rain-water falling upon the roof of a house Rows down to the ground through spouts grotesquely shaped like the tiger's head, thus seeming to come out of tigers' mouths, while in reality it descends from the sky; even so are the holy instructions that come out of the mouths of godly men, which seem to be uttered by those men themselves, while in reality they proceed from the throne of God. (See 225.)

298. As it is very difficult to gather together the mustard-seeds that escape out of a torn package, and are scattered in all directions; so, when the human mind runs in diverse directions and is occupied with many things in the world, it is not a very easy affair to collect and concentrate it.

299. As thieves cannot enter the house the inmates of which are wide awake, so, if you are always on your guard, no

evil spirits will be able to enter your heart to rob it of its goodness.

300. The new-born calf looks very lively, blithe, and merry. It jumps and runs all day long, and only stops to suck the sweet milk from its darn. But no sooner is the rope placed round its neck than it begins to pine away gradually, and, far from being merry, wears a dejected and sorry appearance, and gets almost reduced to a skeleton. So long as a boy has no concern with the affairs of the world he is as merry as the day is long. But when he once feels the weight of the responsibilities of a man of family, by binding himself in time to the world by the indissoluble tie of wedlock, then he no longer appears jolly, but wears the look of dejection, care, and anxiety, and is seen to lose the glow of health from his cheeks, while wrinkles gradually make their appearance over the forehead. Blessed is he that remains a boy throughout his life, free as the morning air, fresh as a newly-blown flower, and pure as a dewdrop.

301. A boat may stay in the water, but water should not stay in the boat. An aspirant may live in the world, but the world should not live in him.

302. He who thinks his spiritual guide a mere man, cannot derive any benefit from him.

303. What you think you should say. Let there be a harmony between your thoughts and your words; otherwise, if you merely tell that God is your all in all, while your mind has made the world its all in all, you cannot derive any benefit thereby.

304. A young plant should be always protected by a fence from the mischief of goats and cows and little urchins. But when once it becomes a big tree, a flock of goats or a herd of cows may find shelter under its spreading boughs, and fill their stomachs with its leaves. So when you have

but little faith within you, you should protect it from the evil influences of bad company and worldliness. But when once you grow strong in faith, no worldliness or evil inclination will dare approach your holy presence; and many who are wicked will become godly through your holy contact.

305. If you wash the body of an elephant and set him at large, he is sure to get himself dirtied in no time, but if after washing him you tie him down to his own room he will remain clean. So if by the good influences of holy men you once become pure in spirit, and then allow yourself the liberty to mix freely with worldly men, you are sure to lose that purity soon; but if you keep your mind fixed on your God, you will never more get soiled in spirit.

306. Where does the strength of an aspirant lie? It is in his tears. As a mother gives her consent to fulfil the desire of her importunately weeping child, so God vouchsafes to His weeping son whatever he is crying for.

307. Meditate on God either in an unknown corner, or in the solitude of forests, or within your own mind.

308. Chant forth the sweet name of Hari (God), keeping time all the while by clapping your hands, then you will acquire mental concentration. If you clap your hands, sitting under a tree, the birds on the boughs thereof will fly away in all directions, and when you chant forth the name of Hari and clap your hands, all evil thoughts will fly away from your mind.

309, 310. As the same fish is dressed into soup, curry, or cutlet, and each has his own choice dish of it, so the Lord of the Universe, though one, manifests Himself differently according to the different likings of His worshippers, and each of these has his own taste of God, which he values the most. To some He is a kind master or a loving father, a sweet smiling mother or a devout friend, and to others a faithful husband or a dutiful and obliging son.

311. Bow down and adore where others kneel, for where so many hearts have been paying the tribute of adoration, the kind Lord will manifest Himself, for He is all mercy.

312. There are men, who, although they have nothing to attract them in this world, create some attachments for themselves, and so try to bind themselves to this earth. They do not want and do not like to be free. A man who has no family to care for, no relatives to look after, generally takes a cat, or a monkey, or a dog, or a bird for a pet object and companion; and thus slakes his thirst for milk by drinking mere whey. Such is the power of Māyā or Nescience over humanity.

313, 314. A patient, in high fever and excess of thirst, imagines that he can drink away quite a sea of water; but when that fit of fever goes and he regains his normal temperature, he can barely quaff off a single cupful of water, and his thirst is at once appeased with even a very small quantity of it. So a man, being under the feverish excitement of Māyā, and forgetful of his own littleness, imagines that he can embrace the whole of Divinity within his own bosom, but when the illusion passes away a single ray of Divine Light is seen to be sufficient to flood him with eternal divine bliss.

315. A man, under the influence of very high fever and in excessive thirst, is placed between a row of pitchers filled with cold water and a set of open-mouthed bottles filled with flavoury sauces. Is it possible for the thirsty and restless patient in such a case to refrain from either drinking the water or from tasting the sauces placed so near him, although thereby his case may become worse? Even such is the case with the man who is under the maddening influence of his ever-active and misleading

senses when he is placed between the attractions of woman's charm on the one side and those of wealth on the other. It is then difficult for him to behave properly, and he is liable to deviate often from the true path and thus make his case worse.

316. None ventures to keep milk in a vessel in which curd had formerly formed, lest the milk itself should get curdled. Nor can the vessel be safely used for other working purposes lest it should crack upon the fire. It is therefore almost useless. A good and experienced preceptor does not entrust to a worldly man valuable and exalting precepts, for he is sure to misinterpret and misuse them to suit his own mean designs. Nor will he ask him to do any useful work that may cost a little labour, lest he should think that the preceptor was taking undue advantage of him.

317. When a certain quantity of pure milk is mixed with double the quantity of water, it takes a long time and much labour to thicken it to the consistency of Kshira (condensed milk). The mind of a worldly man is largely diluted with the filthy water of evil and impure thoughts, and it requires much time and labour before anything can be done to purify and give the proper consistency to it.

318. The vanities of all others may gradually die out, but the vanity of a saint as regards his sainthood is hard indeed to wear away.

319. Of the grains of paddy which are fried in a frying-pan, the few which leap out of the pan and burst outside are the best fried, being without the slightest mark of any tinge; while every one of the properly-fried grains in the pan itself is sure to have at least a very small charred mark of a burn. So of all good devotees, the few who altogether give up the world and go out of it are perfect without any spot, while even the best of those devotees who are in the

world must have at least some small spot of imperfection in their character.

320. We cannot say that God is gracious because He feeds us, for every father is bound to supply his children with food; but when He keeps us from going astray, and holds us back from temptations, then He is truly gracious.

321. If you can detect and find out the universal illusion or Māyā,, it will fly away from you, just as a thief runs away when found out.

322. Fire itself has no definite shape, but in glowing embers it assumes certain forms, and the formless fire is then endowed with forms. Similarly, the formless God sometimes invests Himself with definite forms.

323. Should we pray aloud unto God? Pray unto Him in any way you like. He is sure to hear you, for He can hear even the footfall of an ant.

324. He who tries to give one an idea of God by mere book-learning is like the man who tries to give one an idea of Kāsī (Benares) by means of a map or a picture.

325. A man began to sink a well, but having dug down to the depth of twenty cubits he could not find the least trace of the water-spring which was to feed his well. So he desisted from the work and selected another place for the purpose. There he dug deeper than before, but even then he could not find any water. So again he selected another spot and dug still deeper than before, but it was also of no avail. At last in utter disgust he gave up the task altogether. The sum total of the depths of these three wells was little short of a hundred cubits. Had he had the patience to devote even a half of the whole of this labour to his first well, without shifting the site of the well from place to place, he would surely have been successful in getting water. Such is the case with men who continually shift their positions in regard to faith. In order to meet with success

we should devote ourselves entirely to a single object of faith, without being doubtful as to its efficacy.

326. Although in a grain of paddy the germ is considered the only necessary thing (for germination and growth), while the husk or chaff is considered to be of no importance, still if the unhusked grain be put into the ground it will not sprout up and grow into a plant and produce rice. To get a crop one must needs sow the grain with the husk on; but if one wants to get at the germinating matter itself he must first perform the operation of removing the husk from the seed. So rites and ceremonies are necessary for the growth and perpetuation of a religion. They are the receptacles that contain the seeds of truth, and consequently every man must perform them before he reaches the central truth.

327. The pearl-oyster that contains the precious pearl is in itself of very little value, but it is essential for the growth of the pearl. The shell itself is of no use to the man who has got the pearl, neither are ceremonies and rites necessary for him who has attained the Highest Truth —God.

328. A woodcutter led a very miserable life with the small means he could procure by daily selling the load of wood brought from a neighbouring forest. Once a Saṃnyāsin, who was wending his way through the forest, saw him at work, and advised him to proceed onward into the interior recesses of the forest, intimating to him that he would be a gainer thereby. The woodcutter obeyed the injunction and proceeded onward till he came to a sandal-wood tree, and being much pleased he took away with him as many sandal-logs as he could carry, and sold them in the market and derived much profit. Then he began to think within himself why the good Saṃnyāsin did not tell him anything about the wood of the sandal-trees, but simply advised him to proceed onward into the interior

of the forest. So the next day he went on even beyond the place of the sandal-wood, and at last came upon a copper-mine, and he took with him as much copper as he could carry, and selling it in the market got much money by it. Next day, without stopping at the copper-mine, he proceeded further still, as the Sādhu had advised him to do, and came upon a silver-mine, and took with him as much of it as he could carry, and sold it all and got even more money; and so daily proceeding further and further he got at gold-mines and diamond-mines, and at last became exceedingly rich. Such is also the case with the man who aspires after true knowledge. If he does not stop in his progress after attaining a few extraordinary and supernatural powers, he at last becomes really rich in the eternal knowledge of truth.

329. If you first smear the palms of your hands with oil and then break open the jack-fruit, the sticky milky exudation of the fruit will not stick to your hands and trouble you. So if you first fortify yourself with the true knowledge of the Universal Self, and then live in the midst of wealth and women, they will affect you in no way.

330. He who would learn to swim must attempt swimming for some days. No one can venture to swim in the sea after a single day's practice. So if you want to swim in the sea of Brahman, you must make many ineffectual attempts at first, before you can successfully swim therein.

331. When does a man get his salvation? When his egoism dies.

332. When a sharp thorn finds its way into the sole of one's foot, one takes another thorn to get the former out, and then casts both of them away. So relative knowledge alone can remove the relative ignorance which blinds the eye of the Self. As both such knowledge and ignorance are comprised truly under Nescience, the man who attains

the highest Jñāna, or knowledge of the Absolute, does away with both knowledge and ignorance in the end, being himself free from all duality.

333. To drink pure water from a shallow pond, one should gently take the water from the surface, and not disturb it. If it is disturbed the sediments will rise up from the bottom and make the whole water muddy. If you desire to be pure, have firm faith and slowly go on with your devotional practices, and waste not your energies in useless scriptural discussions and arguments. The little brain will otherwise be muddled.

334. If this body is worthless and transitory, why do pious and devout men take care of it? No one takes care of an empty box. All protect with care a chest full of precious jewels, gold, and costly articles. The pious soul cannot help taking care of the body in which the Divine one dwells, for all our bodies form the playground of the Deity.

335. The tender bamboo can be easily bent, but the full-grown bamboo breaks when an attempt is made to bend it. It is easy to bend young hearts towards good, but the heart of the old escapes the hold when so drawn.

336. The locomotive engine easily drags along a train of heavily-laden carriages. So the loving children of God, firm in their faith and devotion to Him, feel no trouble in passing through all the worries and anxieties of life, and leading many men along with them to God.

337. Every man should follow his own religion. A Christian should follow Christianity, a Mohammedan should follow Mohammedanism, and so on. For the Hindus the ancient path, the path of the Aryan Rishis, is the best.

338, 339. He alone is the true man who is illumined with the light of true knowledge. Others are men in name only.

340. The magnetic needle always points towards the North, and hence it is that the sailing-vessel does not lose her course. So long as the heart of man is directed towards God he cannot be lost in the ocean of worldliness.

341. As the village maidens in India carry four or five pots of water placed one over the other upon their heads, talking all the way with one another about their own joys and sorrows, and yet do not allow one drop of water to be spilt, so must the traveller in the path of virtue walk along. In whatever circumstances he may be placed, let him always take heed that his heart does not swerve from the true path.

342. In our theatrical exhibitions wherein the life and exploits of Krishna are exhibited, the performance commences with the beating of drums and the singing aloud of 'O Krishna, come; come, O dear one.' But the person who plays the part of Krishna pays no heed to this noise and turmoil, and goes on complacently chatting and smoking in the green-room behind the stage. But as soon as the noise ceases, and the pious sage Nārada enters on the stage with sweet and soft music and calls upon Krishna to come out with a heart overflowing with love, Krishna finds that he can no longer remain indifferent, and hurriedly comes on to the stage. So long as the religious devotee cries, 'Come, O Lord; come, O Lord,' with lip-prayers only, verily the Lord will never come; when the Lord does come, the heart of the devotee will melt in divine emotion, and his loud utterances will all cease for ever. The Lord cannot delay in coming when man calls upon Him from the depths of his heart overflowing with deep love and devotion.

343. There is no Path safer and smoother than that of ba-kalamā (*sic*). Ba-kalamā means resigning the self to the will of the Almighty, to have no consciousness that anything is 'mine.'

344. What is the nature of absolute reliance? It is that happy state of comfort felt by a fatigued worker, when reclining on a pillow he smokes at leisure after a hard day's toil: it is a cessation of all anxieties and worries.

345. As dry leaves are blown about here and there by the wind, and have no choice of their own, and make no exertion: so those who depend upon God move in harmony with His will, and can have no will, and put forth no effort, of their own.

346, 347. What do you think of the man who is a good orator and preacher, but whose spirituality is undeveloped? He is like a person who squanders another's property left in trust with him. He can easily advise others, for it costs him nothing, as the ideas he expresses are not his own, but borrowed.

348. A worldly man is best known by his antipathy to whatever savours of religion. He does not like to hear any sacred music or psalm, or to utter the holy name of God, and even dissuades others from doing the same. He scoffs at prayers, and pours down a volley of abuse upon all religious societies and men.

349. As a boy holding on to a post or a pillar gyrates round it with headlong speed without fear of a fall, so, fixing thy hold firmly on God, perform thy worldly duties, and thou shalt be free from all dangers.

350. As an unchaste woman, busily engaged in household affairs, is all the while thinking of her secret lover, even so, O thou man of the world, do thy round of worldly duties, but fix thy heart always on the Lord.

351. As a wet-nurse in a rich family brings up the child of her master, loving the baby as if it were her own, but knows well that she has no claim upon it; so think ye also that you are but trustees and guardians of your children whose real father is the Lord God in Heaven.

352. It is useless to pore over holy scriptures and sacred Shastras without a discriminating and dispassionate mind. No spiritual progress can be made without discrimination (Viveka) and dispassion (Vairāgya).

353. Know thyself, and thou shalt then know the non-self and the Lord of all. What is my ego? Is it my hand, or foot, or flesh, or blood, or muscle, or tendon? Ponder deep, and thou shalt know that there is no such thing as I. As by continually peeling off the skin of the onion, so by analysing the ego it will be found that there is not any real entity corresponding to the ego. The ultimate result of all such analysis is God. When egoism drops away, Divinity manifests itself.

354. The truly devotional and spiritual practice suited for this Iron-age (Kālī-yuga) is the constant repetition of the name of the Lord of Love.

355. If thou wishest to see God, have firm faith in the efficacy of repeating the name of Hari, and try to discriminate the real from the unreal.

356. When an elephant is let loose, it goes about uprooting trees and shrubs, but as soon as the driver pricks him on the head with the goad he becomes quiet; so the mind when unrestrained wantons in the luxuriance of idle thoughts, but becomes calm at once when struck with the goad of discrimination.

357. Devotional practices are necessary only so long as tears of ecstasy do not flow at hearing the name of Hari. He needs no devotional practices whose heart is moved to tears at the mere mention of the name of Hari.

358. The companionship of the holy and wise is one of the main elements of spiritual progress.

359. The soul reincarnates in a body of which it was thinking just before its last departure from this world. Devotional

practices may therefore be seen to be very necessary. When, by constant practice, no worldly ideas arise in the mind, then the god-idea alone fills the soul, and does not leave it even when on the brink of eternity.

360. How should one love God? As the true and chaste wife loves her husband and the niggardly miser loves his hoarded wealth, so the devotee should love the Lord with all his heart and soul.

361. How may we conquer the old Adam in us? When the fruit grows out of the flower, the petals of the flower drop off of themselves. So, when the divinity in thee increases, the weaknesses of thy human nature will all vanish of their own accord.

362, 363. When does the attraction of sensual and worldly pleasures die away? In God, who is Indivisible Ever-Existing Bliss, there is a consolidation of all happiness and of all pleasures. They who enjoy Him can find no attraction in the cheap and worthless pleasures of the world.

364. In what condition of the mind does God-vision take place? God is seen when the mind is tranquil. When the mental sea is agitated by the wind of desires, it cannot reflect God, and then God-vision is impossible.

365. How may we find our God? The angler, anxious to hook a big and beautiful Rohitta-fish, waits calmly for hours together, having thrown the bait and the hook into the water, watching patiently until the bait is caught by the fish. Similarly, the devotee who patiently goes on with his devotions is sure at last to find his God.

366. The heart of a sinner is like a curled hair. You may pull it ever so long, but will not succeed in making it straight. So also the heart of the wicked cannot be easily changed.

367. Knowledge leads to unity, and Ignorance to diversity.

368, 369. The society of pious men is like the water in which rice is washed. The rice-water dissipates intoxication. So doth the society of the pious relieve worldly men, intoxicated with the wine of desires, from their intoxication.

370. The agent of a rich Zemindar, when he goes into the mofussil or interior, tyrannises in various ways over the tenants. But when he comes back to the head-quarters under the eyes of his master, he changes his ways, becomes very pious, treats the tenants kindly, inquires fully into all their grievances, and tries to mete out impartial justice to all. The tyrannical agent even becomes good through the fear of the landlord, and by the effect of his society. Similarly doth the society of the pious make even the wicked righteous, awakening awe and reverence within them.

371. Moist wood placed upon a fire soon becomes dry, and ultimately begins to burn. Similarly, the society of the pious drives away the moisture of greed and lust from the hearts of worldly men and women, and then the fire of Viveka (Discrimination) burns in them.

372. How should one pass his or her life? As the fire on the hearth is stirred from time to time with a poker to make it burn brightly and prevent it from going out, so the mind should be invigorated occasionally by the society of the pious.

373. As the blacksmith keeps alive the fire of his furnace by the occasional blowing of his bellows, so the mind should be kept a-burning by the society of the pious.

374. Throw an unbaked cake of flour into hot ghee, it will make a sort of boiling noise. But the more it is fried, the less becomes the noise; and when it is fully fried the bubbling ceases altogether. So long as a man has little knowledge, he goes about lecturing and preaching, but when the

perfection of knowledge is obtained, he ceases to make vain displays.

375. That man who, living in the midst of the temptations of the world, attains perfection, is the true hero.

376. We must dive deep into the ocean of the Eternal-Intelligent-Bliss. Fear not the deep-sea monsters, Avarice and Anger. Coat thyself with the turmeric of Discrimination and Dispassion (Viveka and Vairāgya) and those alligators will not approach thee, as the scent of this turmeric is too much for them.

377. When unavoidably entering into places where there may be temptation, carry always with thee the thought of thy Divine Mother. She will protect thee from the many evils that may be lurking even in thy heart. Cannot the presence of thy mother shame thee away from evil deeds and evil thoughts?

378. How may we conquer the love of life? The human frame is made up of decaying things; of flesh and blood and bone. It is a collection of flesh, bone, marrow, blood, and other filthy substances subject to putrefaction. By thus analysing the body, our love thereof vanishes.

379. Should the devotee adopt any particular costume? The adoption of a suitable costume is good. Dressed in the Samnyâsin's orange robes, or carrying the religious mendicant's tambourine and cymbals, a man can never utter light and profane things, or sing profane songs. But a man dressed in the smart style of a beau will naturally have his heart inclined to think low thoughts and sing low songs.

380. Sometimes peace reigns in the heart, but why does it not always last long? The fire made by the burning of the bamboo is soon extinguished unless kept alive by constant blowing. Continual devotion is necessary to keep alive the fire of spirituality.

381. Those who live in the world and try to find salvation are like soldiers that fight protected by the breastwork of a fort, while the ascetics who renounce the world in search of God are like soldiers fighting in the open field. To fight from within the fort is safer than to fight in the open field. (Is this right or should it be transposed?)

382. Pray to the Divine Mother in this wise. Give me, O Mother! love that knows no incontinence, and faith adamantine that cannot be shaken.

383. As persons living in a house infested by venomous snakes are always alert and cautious, so should men living in the world be always on their guard against the allurements of lust and greed.

384. If there is a small hole in the bottom of a jar of water, the whole water flows out of it by that small aperture. Similarly, if there be the smallest tinge of worldliness in the neophyte, all his exertions come to naught.

385. When the butter is produced by churning the whey, it should not be kept in the same vessel containing the remaining whey, for then it will lose something of its sweetness and cohesion. It should be kept in pure water and in a different vessel. So after attaining some partial perfection in the world, if one still continues to mix with the worldly, and remains in the midst of the world, it is likely that he will be tainted; but he will remain pure if he lives out of it.

386. You cannot live in a sooty room without blackening your body to some extent, however small it may be, with all your caution. So, if a man or a woman lives in the company of one of his or her opposite sex of the same age, with the greatest circumspection and control over his or her passion, still some carnal thought, however small, is sure to arise in his or her mind.

387. Two persons, it is said, began together the rite of invoking the Goddess Kālī by the terrible process called 'Savasādhana', (This Tantrik invocation is performed in the cemetery yard, the invoker sitting on the body of a corpse in a dark night.) One invoker was frightened to insanity by the horrors of the earlier portion of the night; the other was favoured with the vision of the Divine Mother at the end of the night. Then he asked her, 'Mother! why did the other man become mad?' The Deity answered, Thou too, O child! didst become mad many times in thy various previous births, and now at last thou seest me.'

388. There are various sects among the Hindus; which sect or which creed should we then adopt? Pārvati once asked Mahādeva, 'O Lord! what is the root of the Eternal, Everlasting, All-embracing Bliss?' To her Mahādeva thus replied, 'The root is faith.' The peculiarities of creeds and sects matter little or nothing. Let every one perform with faith the devotions and the duties of his own creed.

389. As a little boy or a girl can have no idea of conjugal affection, even so a worldly man cannot at all comprehend the ecstasy of Divine communion.

390. The body is transient and unimportant. Why then is it so much looked after? No one cares for an empty box. But people carefully preserve the box that contains money and other valuable property. The virtuous cannot but take care of the body, the temple of the soul in which God has manifested Himself or which has been blessed by God's advent.

391. How long does godliness remain in man? The iron is red so long as it is in fire. It is black the moment it is removed from fire. So the human being is godly so long as he is in communion with God.

392. Soft clay admits of forms, but the burnt clay does not. So those whose hearts are consumed with the desire of worldly things cannot realise higher ideas.

393. As the water and its bubbles are one, and as the bubbles have their birth in the water, float on the water, and ultimately are resolved into water; so the Gīvātman and the Paramātman are one and the same: the difference is in degrees—the one is finite and small, the other is infinite; the one is dependent, the other independent.

394, 395. When the tail of the tadpole drops off, it can live both in water and on land. When the tail of ignorance drops off, man becomes free. He can then live both in God and in the world equally well.